Walt Whitman's
NEW ORLEANS

Library of Southern Civilization

Oldest known daguerreotype of Walt Whitman,
likely produced in New Orleans in 1848.

Walt Whitman's
NEW ⊕ ORLEANS

Sidewalk Sketches & Newspaper Rambles

Edited, with an Introduction, by Stefan Schöberlein

LOUISIANA STATE UNIVERSITY PRESS

BATON ROUGE

Published with the assistance of the V. Ray Cardozier Fund

Published by Louisiana State University Press
lsupress.org

Manufactured in the United States of America
First printing

DESIGNER: Michelle A. Neustrom
TYPEFACE: Calluna
PRINTER AND BINDER: Sheridan Books, Inc.

JACKET ILLUSTRATION: St. Charles Exchange Hotel, New Orleans, 1842, from a
lithograph by B. W. Thayer and Co. The Charles L. Franck Studio Collection at
The Historic New Orleans Collection, 1979.325.4596.

LIBRARY OF CONGRESS CATALOGING-IN-PUBLICATION DATA

Names: Whitman, Walt, 1819–1892, author. | Schöberlein, Stefan, editor.
Title: Walt Whitman's New Orleans : sidewalk sketches and newspaper rambles /
    edited, with an introduction, by Stefan Schöberlein.
Description: Baton Rouge : Louisiana State University Press, [2022] | Series: Library of
    Southern civilization | Includes bibliographical references and index.
Identifiers: LCCN 2021024321 (print) | LCCN 2021024322 (ebook) | ISBN 978-0-8071-
    7682-5 (cloth) | ISBN 978-0-8071-7723-5 (pdf) | ISBN 978-0-8071-7724-2 (epub)
Subjects: LCSH: Whitman, Walt, 1819–1892—Homes and haunts—Louisiana—New
    Orleans. | New Orleans (La.)—In literature. | Crescent City (New Orleans, La.)
Classification: LCC PS3203 .S36 2022 (print) | LCC PS3203 (ebook) | DDC
    818/.309—dc23
LC record available at https://lccn.loc.gov/2021024321
LC ebook record available at https://lccn.loc.gov/2021024322

———— ✦ ————

Being now out of a job, I was offer'd impromptu, (it happen'd between the acts one night in the lobby of the old Broadway theatre near Pearl street, New York city,) a good chance to go down to New Orleans on the staff of the "Crescent," a daily to be started there with plenty of capital behind it. One of the owners, who was north buying material, met me walking in the lobby, and though that was our first acquaintance, after fifteen minutes' talk (and a drink) we made a formal bargain, and he paid me two hundred dollars down to bind the contract and bear my expenses to New Orleans. I started two days afterwards; had a good leisurely time, as the paper wasn't to be out in three weeks. I enjoy'd my journey and Louisiana life much.

—WALT WHITMAN, *Specimen Days*

———— ✦ ————

CONTENTS

The Daily Crescent

FIFTEEN CENTS A WEEK. SUNDAY MORNING, MARCH 5, 1848. VOLUME I......NUM

DAILY CRESCENT.

Mexican Correspondence.

[CORRESPONDENCE OF THE CRESCENT.]

CITY OF MEXICO, Feb. 12, 1848.

...

Northern Correspondence.

NEW YORK, Feb. 22, 1848.

Friends of the Crescent:—As it cannot but be supposed that not and your readers will be so busy from New York, and the papers are and rumors thick...

Washington Correspondence.

[Correspondence of the Crescent.]

WASHINGTON, February 23, 1848.

Congress has entered upon the fifth week of the session and made such progress in the public business that a brief estimate of proceedings may not be uninteresting to the readers of your newspaper...

PREFACE

L ike most newspapermen writing before the 1860s, Whitman did not sign
his contributions to the *Crescent.* This edition bases its selection of texts
on a number of factors: a history of attribution by Whitman scholars (especially Emory Holloway and the editorial team of Whitman's edited *Journalism*),
initials that point to Whitman, references to events described in his brother's
letters, echoes of other pieces by Whitman, and Whitman's later recollections
about topics covered in his writings. In addition, all texts that feature a coher-
ent narrative persona that echoes Whitman's—one that speaks in New York
slang and/or a suggests being a stranger from the North, traversing New Orleans by foot—were attributed to Whitman.

Furthermore, the complete set of texts contained in this volume was posi-
tively attributed using a computational stylometric approach. For more information on this method, see the essay "Glorious times for newspaper editors
and correspondents," coauthored by the editor, that is recommended at the
end of this volume.

This book is a reader's edition and as such does not aim for comprehensive-
ness but for thematic cohesion. A number of editorials known to be Whitman's—
such as theater reviews, political commentary, or treatises on education—have
been excluded since their primary preoccupation is not directly with the city
and people of New Orleans.

The texts at hand largely retain historical spelling and grammatical oddi-
ties, but all obvious errors (missing words, characters, or spaces, flipped letters,
etc.) have been corrected. The order of texts here generally corresponds to the
chronology of their original print run in the *Crescent,* with some allowances
made for narrative cohesion and flow of the overall volume.

For a more comprehensive edition of Whitman's writings for the *Crescent,*
the editor of this book recommends the forthcoming third volume of *Walt
Whitman: The Journalism* (Peter Lang). The editor extends his warmest thanks

to the surviving team behind *The Journalism,* Zachary Turpin and Jason Stacy, whose feedback was instrumental in assembling this collection, and expresses his condolences over the passing of their colleague Doug Noverr. Doug's imprint on the scholarship of Whitman's journalism looms large, and he will be sorely missed.

The editor of this volume also gratefully acknowledges the Walt Whitman Archive (www.whitmanarchive.org), which is in the process of making all of Whitman's writings, including his early work, available online to scholars and general readers, free of charge.

INTRODUCTION

Whitman on the Levee

O ne has to wonder what impressions ran through the head of young jour-
nalist Walter Whitman as he first stepped off the boat in New Orleans
on a pleasant, late-February night in 1848. Just twenty-eight years old and
with his teenage brother, Jeff, in tow, Whitman had just completed a roughly
fifteen-hundred-mile trip—by train, stagecoach, and boat—through what was
then the American West. It was the first time that the former schoolteacher
had left New York. Crossing the vast country had been an adventure for the
young writer. Dialects on deck, regional meals, the rugged charm of the folks
"out West"—all of it had felt invigorating and new.

Still, Whitman was no country bumpkin. In New York City and Brooklyn, he had been a well-known newspaperman, often seen strolling through
the boroughs twirling his walking cane and occasionally fighting with fellow editors, both in print and with fisticuffs. A towering figure, with prema-
turely graying hair, he was a proper "man about town"—as much dandy as
self-educated street tough. Until a few weeks prior, he had been the editor of
the *Brooklyn Daily Eagle,* a major paper of the then-independent city. In that
position, he had penned fiery lead articles lambasting the cultural and political
establishment, which often triggered vehement rebuttals from the print com-
petition. In his roughly fifteen years in the business, Walter Whitman had also
published a number of sensational, at times sentimental, stories and poems
that sold well. And his first novel, *Franklin Evans* (1842), a work of temperance
fiction, had been quite popular with readers. Walter certainly would have considered himself a rising star.

His exact reasons for quitting Brooklyn to help start a paper in New Orleans are somewhat shrouded in mystery. Whitman himself would later claim
he left on a whim after a happenstance conversation with one of his future employers during the intermission at a local theater. It is more likely that some-

body associated with the *Eagle* helped facilitate the trip. Whatever was the case, going to New Orleans surely looked like a good prospect, professionally and personally. The new paper he was to help found was the *Daily Crescent*—the Long Island native's next big project.

Whitman must have had some inkling what New Orleans might be like. Writing for the *Eagle,* he would have encountered the city in its pages as a distant gateway to the battlefields of Mexico and the gold mines of California. As the largest city in the South, it was a place of trade, fortune seeking, military excursion but also of yellow fever and cholera. It had seen military luminaries like Andrew Jackson, Henry Clay, and Zachary Taylor walk its streets. It was also the home of the *New Orleans Delta,* which the *Eagle* quoted frequently in its pages and whose cofounders had invited Whitman to be a part of their latest journalistic venture.

Whatever the young writer knew, the city undoubtedly felt quite foreign on that night in late February. Gazing straight ahead from Poydras Street Wharf, suitcases in hand, the Whitman brothers caught a first glance of the bustling heart of New Orleans, shimmering in the gaslight. Unlike New York, the Crescent City had seen only one great fire—in the eighteenth century—and much of its colonial architecture remained intact. While the visual iconography of New Orleans is widely known today, that was not the case in Whitman's time: the shotgun houses of the city's faubourgs, the abundant peach blossoms and live oaks covered in Spanish moss, the ornate balconies of the French Quarter, the densely populated, above-ground cemeteries—Whitman would have been little prepared for the barrage of new impressions. Aside from a drawing or two in a monthly magazine, perhaps of the 1815 Battle of New Orleans, Whitman had likely never encountered detailed depictions of the city.

In this exotic metropolis of the South, Whitman observed, many people spoke variants of French or conversed in Spanish. He had experienced his share of linguistic mixing and slang back home, but this felt different. While New Orleans had been part of the United States for almost five decades, French culture was still dominant here and would have felt foreign to the New Yorker of Dutch Quaker heritage. Many laws and regulations still echoed Napoleonic Code, and customs were quite different from stiff, northern Yankeedom. The idea of racial mixing—something Whitman had toyed with in *Franklin Evans*—was embodied in the Crescent City, omnipresent and multifaceted. New Orleans not only showed Whitman the horrors of slavery but also hinted at the possibilities of Black citizenship as practiced in creole culture and by the freedpeople thriving in the city. Even local religion felt strange: Catholicism, largely associated in New York with recent Irish immigration (and as such, skeptically eyed by Whitman), had a history in New Orleans that predated the town itself and dominated religious practice. Mardi Gras, Whitman would comment, felt outright devilish.

Of course, there were also the less mind-boggling culture shocks: even compared to New York, New Orleans *stank*. "It is a very dirty place," brother Jeff would complain to their mother, "I never wanted your cleanliness so much before." Especially their first boardinghouse—located on the corner of Poydras and St. Charles streets—did not compare to the luxuries of steamboat life: "you could not only see the dirt, but you could taste it, and you had to, too, if you ate anything at all," the teenager bemoaned. Luckily, the brothers quickly moved on to more comfortable lodgings just a few buildings over, likely with some help of Walter's employers, who may have been friends with his new landlord.

————— ✦ —————

With better housing secured, the two Whitmans soon began their work for the *Daily Crescent*. Jeff became the office boy and expressed satisfaction with his tasks and relatively high wages, though his brother would later complain about the teenager's workload. Much of Jeff's time was spent carrying newspapers to and from the post office. Walter himself took on the role as the paper's "exchange editor" and contributed pieces on education and democratic politics, wrote theater reviews, and penned short *flâneur* prose. Contemporary reviews of the paper suggest Walter's contributions to be substantial, one even putting him "in charge" of the paper. The brothers shared an office space with five other men in a large complex of buildings across from their hotel. A painting of the German poet-philosopher Schiller graced the office walls, and Lafayette Square could be seen from the window. The incessant noise of St. Charles Street below was deafening.

The newsroom was led by an experienced proprietor couple: Alexander Hamilton Hayes, fifteen years Whitman's senior, and John Eliot McClure, in his late twenties. Both were born in New England but had been well-known figures in New Orleans's publishing scene for years. They were hands-on newspapermen but did not contribute much writing: Hayes was responsible for the paper's design and layout while McClure served as business manager. Later a tax collector and freelance accountant, J. O. Pierson, would join the paper's leadership, largely as a financial investor.

Hayes and McClure knew what they were doing: even in the crowded newspaper space of New Orleans, their startup soon became a household staple—the locals liked it, even when not a single staff member was native to Louisiana. Not only was the paper well produced but, at eight dollars a year, it was quite affordable. The *Crescent* also received positive nods from other papers across the country, though in its editorials it would complain about being sidelined by some national publications until the end of 1848. "Really, Gentlemen, some of your compliments quite make us blush," the *Crescent* performatively informed its northern colleagues just three weeks after its first issue. Whitman himself, it seems, was one of the reasons readers were drawn to the paper. While none of his contributions were clearly attributed at the time (aside from an occasional "W." or "W.W."), Whitman identified himself as "You know who" or playfully alluded to his status as a stranger from New York. Clearly, readers were in on the joke.

The bulk of the daily writing duty was shared between Whitman and two colleagues: George W. Reeder and John C. Larue. The former, an Irish nationalist, was the city news reporter and would spend a lot of time at the Recorder's Courts, drafting mocking, satirical portraits of defendants and their alleged misdeeds. Reeder may have also contributed some short fiction. Laure, on the other hand, had little patience for literary fancy or humor. The New Jersey native was a local attorney, a former military advisor, and had ambitions to branch into Democratic politics. His caustic style was widely known. Though admired by Whitman, Laure failed to gain popularity as a writer and politician, which his own obituaries connected to a vinegary personality. Laure lectured on the French Revolution on his own time, and likely contributed a number of editorial pieces on the republican revolutions in Europe as well as US-Mexican politics.

There was also Durant DaPonte—a descendent of a famous opera singer, multilinguist, and just three years older than Jeff—who was tasked with translation and miscellanea. In addition, he appears to have authored some poems for the *Crescent* as "D." Later, he would become a Klansman. Other occasional contributions included letters by a solid roster of long-term correspondents as well as poems by Brooklynite Thomas A. Gould, Matt Field (uncle of journalism icon Kate Field), and an Irish sailor going by the name "Jack Waterways," who was said to drop off verses when on shore leave (and may just have been a fanciful persona of a local writer).

———— + ————

Whitman's workday would begin around 9:00 a.m. Upon his arrival, papers from the big cities up north would be waiting for him. These periodicals received preferential treatment by the postal service and could be mailed by their proprietors at a significantly reduced rate. Quickly, the first pages of the *Crescent* were dominated by clippings from his hometown papers, selected and commented on by Whitman. For all intents and purposes, Whitman became the voice of the *Crescent*'s news, speaking in a kind of cut-out collage. In contrast to journalistic standards of today, color commentary was expected and encouraged even in news sections. Papers celebrated their political biases, often running political ads in their headers, and an editor like Whitman would slander, quip, and sermonize while presenting the latest goings-on from the Northeast—"latest," of course, translating to a postal delay of ten to fifteen days.

Whitman had performed similar tasks as the editor of other papers, but being a newsman was certainly not his primary qualification for the *Crescent* job. Consequently, an interested reader could also find much more distinctly Whitmanian contributions in the paper. One of the specialties of the young writer were "peeps" and sidewalk observations. In these pieces, Whitman perambulated the metropolis while taking his readers with him, presenting them with the working-class sights of the town, humorously intensifying characters they might meet in a particular neighborhood, and describing the populace flowing like a river up and down the city's streets. He had composed pieces like these in New York and now discovered this genre to be a good fit for his New Orleans writings. In this way, Whitman introduced readers to the city; even those who knew the place intimately could experience it afresh through Whitman's eyes.

After work, the two Whitmans would set out exploring the vibrant, multitudinous city, soaking up impressions for Walter's pen. From their lodgings in what is today the central business district, most major cultural sites were only a brisk walk away. Jeff and Walter visited Catholic cemeteries, observed parades, walked the levee, attended the theater, and—Jeff at least—eyed elaborately dressed ladies walking down the broad avenues. Whitman's writings disclose a heightened interested in "juleps," masked balls, and the rowdy bars around the St. Charles Hotel.

New Orleans in these days was flush with young men from all over the nation: soldiers who had bonded during the recent US-Mexico War and were now let loose on the city to celebrate their victory; eager traders trying to make it big in the booming hub; fortune seekers on route to gold country via South America. Whitman is perhaps a bit coy in his New Orleans recollections (in the epilogue of this volume), but an associate, the aforementioned Thomas A. Gould, is more forthcoming. In a later series for the *Brooklyn Daily Eagle*, Gould, who may have had a hand in getting Whitman his job down south, recounts the nightlife of New Orleans in this way: "Sitting, standing, walking, talking, smiling, laughing, lolling, leaning, thinking, swearing, strolling and drinking, were representatives from every part of the world. The exemplary and the profligate—priests, pirates, statesmen, fops, fools, gamblers, gold diggers, etc., etc., all mingled in most grotesque confusions. Embryo heroes, en route to Mexico, conversing with pomp of vanity, with old, tired, battle-scarred veterans. Hoosiers, also, with rough coats, gaping mouths, staring eyes, and independent stride. City merchants, in groups discoursing of trade. Little knots of blustering bravos, 'mysteriously affectionate.'"

One can almost see "confirmed bachelor" Gould wink when he places quotation marks around that last phrase. Gould (born around 1820) was a Brooklyn poet and painter who stayed in New Orleans at the same time as the Whitman brothers, and his work was frequently promoted by the *Crescent* during Whitman's tenure. Scholarship now generally agrees that the poet had at least one romantic relationship with another man at the time, an experience which likely yielded the "Calamus Leaves" manuscript (in the epilogue of this volume). Though the identity of the person(s) in question remains unclear, it makes sense that Whitman would have experienced his time in New Orleans as sexually liberating.

New Orleans at the nexus of gold rush, immigration, war, and trade created a fertile playground for a variety of "mysterious affections" between men. What Whitman would later call "adhesiveness"—his term for male-male love borrowed from the pseudoscience of phrenology—was on full display in the Crescent City. Prior to the existence of a modern concept of homosexuality (as sexual orientation), hand-holding, embracing, or sharing a bed were broadly considered appropriate expressions of bonding between members of the same sex. A city like New Orleans, overrun with transitory young men of marriageable age without local family ties, invited further experimentation. When Whitman was pressed, late in life, about his sexual history in New Orleans, he became flustered, quickly making up stories about affairs with women and having fathered numerous illegitimate children. The vehemence of his old-age denials suggests both an awareness of the growing homophobia of the 1890s and a conscious desire to rewrite this particular part of his biography.

In Whitman's writings in and about New Orleans, the kind of men Whitman was attracted to can be found scattered over almost every page, be they oyster vendors, omnibus drivers, or street toughs. Their type struck Whitman's fancy—personally and politically. In a poem that would ultimately be called "I Dreamed in a Dream" (part of "Calamus Leaves" in the epilogue), Whitman imagines the male-male culture of queer New Orleans as a political program:

I dreamed in a dream of a city where all the men were like brothers,
O I saw them tenderly love each other—I often saw them, in numbers,
    walking hand in hand;
I dreamed that was the city of robust friends—Nothing was greater there
    than manly love—it led the rest,
It was seen every hour in the actions of the men of that city, and in all
    their looks and words.

In these lines Whitman envisions a sort of homoerotic utopia built on the free association of working men: a robust republic of friends.

———— + ————

I n terms of more pragmatic politics, the radical "Barnburner" wing of the Democratic Party was closest to Whitman's heart at the time. After being driven out by conservative forces, it ran a mildly popular but ultimately unsuccessful third-party bid in 1848 under the banner of the Free Soil Party. Skeptical of big banks, monopolies, and government bureaucracy, the working-class movement attracted Whitman with its promise of "free soil, free speech, free labor, and free men." These populist firebrands, like Whitman, opposed the extension of slavery (for instance into newly acquired Mexican territory), though not primarily on abolitionist grounds but more to protect white labor from having to compete with it. In the process, they often veered into outright nativism. Whitman had been an active, antiestablishment Democrat since his youth and would serve as a Free Soil delegate upon his return from New Orleans. While Whitman's writings produced in New Orleans—frustratingly— are largely silent on the issue of slavery, his general political imprint could still be felt years later. An 1870s piece about one of Whitman's coworkers recalls the somewhat puzzling political leanings of the *Crescent.* In the late 1840s, while disavowing party politics on the surface, it was understood "to advocate Free Soil Doctrine, and yet the editors were intensely Southern."

Besides concrete political positions, the Barnburner movement celebrated a workingman's aesthetic that held strong appeal for the future poet of *Leaves of Grass* (1855). It was a group of activists that *behaved and looked* as radical as their ideas felt. The queer poet and future acquaintance of Whitman, Fitz-Greene Halleck, frames their rough-and-tumble attitude as follows in a poem quoted in one of Whitman's sketches for the *Crescent:*

> 'T is a rough land of earth, and stone, and tree,
>   Where breathes no castled lord or cabined slave;
> Where thoughts, and tongues, and hands are bold and free,
>   And friends will find a welcome, foes a grave;

And where none kneel, save when to Heaven they pray,
Nor even then, unless in their own way.

Theirs is a pure republic, wild, yet strong,
A "fierce democracie," where all are true
To what themselves have voted—right or wrong—
And to their laws, denominated blue;

Barnburnerism became a cultural expression as much as a political program: to Whitman it always also meant a working-class chic, American slang,
and manliness. In a letter to the *Crescent*, sent shortly after his return to New
York, Whitman put it thusly:

The principal beauty of our "Barnburner" friends, consists in their delightful,
youthful, aspect of defiance—quite picturesque and refreshing to one's tired
consciousness. . . . Nothing will please them—these don't-care-a-damnative
young men. They reject advice, and insult even the senators and venerable
editors who give it. They seem to glory in kicking up the most precious of
rows—in rebelling against all the political etiquette of the last thirty years.
Then the ease and complacency of the rascals—with what cool vanity they
dare their elders and superiors in station, to do battle with them—either in
argument or any other way. It is amazing!

Whitman's infatuation with subcultural style and rebellious attitude
alongside traditional armchair politics suggests an early inkling of a notion
that would follow him for the rest of his life: the idea that *being democratic*, ultimately, entails something much more radical than mere voting. Republicanism, Whitman's *Leaves of Grass* would later proclaim, is an egalitarian practice,
not a set of institutions.

———— ✦ ————

I n contrast to the volatile global politics of 1848, Whitman celebrates his
republicanism in his writings for the *Crescent* primarily as tough attitude,

loose tongue, and a working-class sense of humor. "I pride myself on being a real humorist underneath everything else," Whitman would later tell one of his closest associates. Perhaps nowhere in Whitman's oeuvre is this attitude more pronounced than in the sketches he produced for the *Crescent*. From a bumbling country boy bewildered by big-city life, to scathing caricatures of old spinsters, to the occasional dirty pun, Whitman hits all the high and low(-brow) notes of popular, mid-century humor.

Whitman's beliefs and political outlook shine through many of these: pretentiousness, affectation, love of dress get ridiculed by his acerbic pen while hard work, shrewdness, and unvarnished self-expression are rewarded with praise and good humor. He quotes the Bible as a source of practical advice, not spiritual truth. The Sabbath he celebrates as a democratic, secular event of high and low intermingling on busy sidewalks. He is not easily scandalized, whether in front of a sex worker, a street urchin, or a pretty maid. Off-the-cuff (and often misremembered) Shakespearean quotes litter his blue-collar portraits; Dryden and Milton help him mock what needs mocking. He would rather slurp a fresh oyster or two with the urban riffraff than brush his teeth like some perfumed European dandy. He's not one for sitting indoors—he takes the city in and by stride.

The protagonists he meets on these walks are never complex psyches, however, but *tropes:* the jolly flatboatman, the vain woman, the sensitive youth, and so forth. Whitman has little patience for following them through plotlines and character development. They are all buoys bobbing in the ocean of the democratic *en masse.* Supported by the pseudoscience of phrenology, which understood minds as a mechanistic combinations of archetypal qualities, Whitman celebrates his protagonists *as* they are and *where* they are. The "conchologist" Timothy Goujon, for instance, might as well do without a name: he is the French Oyster Peddler. Never more, never less. Goujon does not need to improve or develop. The young writer's inability to envision believable interpersonal conflict or realistic characters is a weakness evident in most of his early prose. His snapshot fiction for the *Crescent,* however, avoids these pitfalls. Instead of emulating the plots and arcs of a Charles Dickens, as he was fond of doing, Whitman is sketching out an impressionistic, humorous way to present New Orleans as a free-flowing constellation of character types, memorable places, and public happenings. In these sketches, working-class fiction meets journalistic "peep" to form a strange, entertaining hybrid.

Ultimately, these characters would inhabit one of Whitman's central, poetic innovations: his so-called catalogs, those long lists of "people doing things" that fill so many pages of *Leaves of Grass.* He is "pleased," Whitman would observe in one of these, with each American, right where they are:

> Pleased with the native and pleased with the foreign. . . . pleased with the
>   new and old,
> Pleased with women, the homely as well as the handsome,
> Pleased with the quakeress as she puts off her bonnet and talks melodiously,
> Pleased with the primitive tunes of the choir of the whitewashed church,
> Pleased with the earnest words of the sweating Methodist preacher. . . .

Surveyed from a distance, the short prose contained in this volume might anticipate these catalogs. They are spotlights of people fully defined and contained by their current state and position—and they are valued as such, without the hackneyed narrative turns common in contemporaneous fiction. Ephraim Broadhorn is interesting without a sudden inheritance plot; Julia Katydid does not require a mysterious curse to make her life enticing; a Sangrado Snipes, for once, can do without getting his just comeuppance. Even the characters Whitman ridicules, belong. Seen together, they portray the republican thrill of a living, breathing New Orleans.

————— ✦ —————

Part of this thrill is racial. Whitman's single substantial comment on the issue is his portrait of Dusky Grisette—a creole sex worker in the guise of a flower girl. Assessment of this sketch has been decidedly mixed, with some academics praising the complexities encoded into the piece while others have condemned it for a lack of sympathy toward her. Certainly, some of the humor that Whitman finds in the very notion of racial mixing—black coffee, white sheets, *brune* skin—feels heartless in a paper that also ran ads for escaped slaves and printed jokes mocking Black women.

In Grisette's sketch, Whitman's authorial perspective moves in and out of the point of view of a white, male customer. In doing so, he speaks the sexual double-standard of the racial politics of New Orleans—the very skin that is so playfully narrated as enticing when dimly illuminated by gaslight serves to mark a subservient status during the day. Racial mixing, embodied in her and practiced with her at night, remains unacknowledged and shunned in the harsh light of the Louisiana sun. The reader is asked to participate in this process and, would the sketch have ended there, might rightly be appalled.

Instead, the narrative follows Grisette further—into her morning shift as a coffee huckster and her afternoon labors as a diligent washerwoman. Grisette's sex work is just that: work. Indeed, she is the hardest worker presented in Whitman's sketches, her day stretching from the early morning hours to late at night without much interruption. If she is a "type" like these other characters, that type is not a "fallen woman." Grisette never quite feels like a caricature— especially when compared to a Virginity Roseblossom or a Giddy Gay Butterfly. Even in his later *Leaves of Grass*, Whitman will denigrate women of Grisette's trade in order to relish pitying them: one might think of the "prostitute that draggles her shawl" with her "bonnet bob[bing] on her tipsy and pimpled neck" in his "Song of Myself." Grisette, on the other hand, is not abject. Nothing about her is "fallen."

Jeff Whitman complained to his mother about all the folks who eagerly hurried to church on Sundays, "dip their fingers in the holy water, and then go home and *whip* their *slaves*." It is frustrating that Walter did not find the courage to bring some of the family's outrage into his work for the *Crescent*. Perhaps Dusky Grisette—marginalized in multiple ways for her gender, race, and labor, but humanized by Whitman—can be read as a conscious political commentary. Even so, it still serves to make the general silence of the elder Whitman feel more deafening.

———————— ✦ ————————

Uneasiness over slavery has thus often been marshaled as one of the reasons the Whitman brothers cut their stay in New Orleans short and returned home after just three months on the job. Whitman himself has put forward a mysterious "coldness" of his editors and a minor payment dispute as an explanation. Some have wondered if his personal relationships may have played a role. Whatever the case, we now know that his split from the paper was not on hostile terms. Instead, as Whitman's own account suggests, there was some negotiation over his leaving—perhaps over the cost of Whitman's journey home—and some continued contributions by Whitman were apparently agreed upon. The poet would continue mailing some of his writings to the paper throughout 1848, including additional installments of his "Sidewalk Sketches" series that have eluded Whitmanites since their initial printing.

In looking back at Whitman's prose in the *Crescent,* much of which is collected here for the first time, the question of quality inevitably comes up. In the last years, each wave of excitement over the discovery of a new Whitman text was quickly followed by some degree of disappointment. Neither *Jack Engle* (1852) nor *Manly Health and Training* (1858), many readers noted, could ultimately compare with *Leaves of Grass.* Whitman's prose, some scholars have even suggested, ought not to be highlighted at all as it deflects from the expressive poetry he has come to be known for. What is the value, then, in reading the impressions of New Orleans by a young Walter Whitman, who was still years away from morphing into the Walt that so many adore today?

One of the beauties of Whitman's New Orleans sketches is that they are exactly that: sketches. They do not espouse a grand political or narrative vision, nor do they attempt to give birth to the next David Copperfield, Natty Bumppo, or Jo March. There are attitudes and ideas simmering in Whitman's style here that make for highly enjoyable reading, even if they had never led to *Leaves.* Whitman aptly maneuvers genre markers from the sentimental to the sensational to summon a charming, complicated, odd picture of a city—a picture painted in curious dots and splashes, not broad strokes. Readers will learn very little about the leading men of town, famous historical conflicts, or the city's role in global trade. Instead, they will discover humorous, deeply proletarian, celebrations of the types of minds and bodies that constitute a place.

Thrown into the situation of having to write for an audience Whitman did not know—and at times literally could not understand—he wrote for a broad audience of Americans: Those that had seen their fair share of a rugged *b'hoys* hanging around at street corners, those who had laughed at the affectations of a dandy gallivanting through muddy streets, and those who had fallen for their share of money-hungry quacks. These figures, common to the American, urban imagination, are the Falstaffs and Dogberrys of this new nation, Whitman suggests, and worthy of as much celebration as those sketched by the Bard of Avon for his Londoners. An American republic needs republican icons—and Whitman in the 1840s was beginning to collect, assemble, and share them.

These sketches, then, are not intended for annotation, interpretation, and close reading; they are meant to be good for a chuckle over a well-crafted pun, for an opportunity to spend a brief moment marveling over the strangeness of human life, or for some glee from the mocking of one's self-proclaimed social betters. These are texts to be enjoyed quickly, while scanning a page of local goings-on, national politics, and advertisements, and while some of this enjoyment might be obscured by references that have aged poorly over the last century and a half, there is still much to attract a busy reader's attention. "Missing me one place, search another," Whitman later recommended to his readers. Perhaps Whitman the humorist is someone we have all missed. Hopefully these sketches will make for a welcome rediscovery of the light-hearted Walt Whitman.

Walt Whitman's
NEW ORLEANS

Approximate travel route of Walt Whitman and his brother
Thomas Jefferson Whitman, to and from New Orleans. MapChart.

PRELUDE

Excerpts from A Traveller's Note Book

—— ✦ ——

Crossing the Alleghanies
SUNDAY, MARCH 5, 1848

We left Baltimore on Saturday morning at seven o'clock, on the railroad for Cumberland, which is about a hundred and seventy miles distant, at the eastern edge of the Alleghanies. Of course, at this season of the year, the country is not remarkably fascinating anywhere; and here a very large portion of the road is bounded on one side or the other by cliffs and steeps of an Alp-like loftiness. We seemed, for at least a hundred miles, to follow the course of an interminable brook, winding with its windings, and twisting with its twists, in a, to me, singular fashion. But even with so many circuits, the road had to be cut through many very bad places; and was probably one of the most expensive railroads ever built. It pays enormous profits, however; and they seriously "talk" about having it continued to some place on the Ohio, perhaps Wheeling, After "talking about it" awhile, it will very likely be done; it only wants money enough—and an enormous lot of that it *will* want, too!

At Harper's Ferry, where they gave us twenty minutes to dine, the scenery is strikingly abrupt and varied. Houses were perched up over our heads— breaks in the ground—and others perched up over *their* heads, and so on. The finest scenery, though, even here, (if it be not a bull to say so,) is about half a mile off. As soon as the cars stopped, a frightful sound of bells and discordant screams surrounded us, and we were all but torn in pieces by assault, as it were! Recovering from the first shock of such an unexpected salute, we found that there were several "hotels," each moved by a bitter rivalry for getting the passengers to eat their dinner. One "opposition house," in particular, seemed

I

bent upon proceeding to extremities—and most of the passengers were fain to go quietly in. For a good dinner here, the price was only twenty-five cents.

Cumberland, at which we arrived about sunset, is a thriving town, with several public edifices, a newspaper or two, and those invariably to be found places in every western and southern community, some big "hotels." The town has a peculiar character, from its being the great rendezvous and ending place of the immense Pennsylvania wagons, and the drovers from hundreds of miles west. You may see Tartar-looking groups of these wagons, and their drivers, in the open grounds about,—the horses being loosed—and the whole having not a little the appearance of a caravan of the Steppes. Hundreds and hundreds of these enormous vehicles, with their arched roofs of white canvas, wend their way into Cumberland from all quarters, during a busy season, with goods to send on eastward, and to take goods brought by the railroad. They are in a shape not a little like the "Chinese junk," whilom exhibited at New York—being built high at each end, and scooping down in the waist. With their teams of four and six horses, they carry an almost incalculable quantity of "freight"; and if one should accidentally get in the road-ruts before their formidable wheels, they would perform the work of Juggernaut upon him in most effectual order. The drivers of these vehicles and the drovers of cattle, hogs, horses, &c., in this section of the land, form a large slice of "society."

Night now falling down around us like a very large cloak of black broadcloth, (I fancy *that* figure, at least, hasn't been used up by the poets,) and the Alleghanies rearing themselves up "some pumpkins," (as they say here,) right before our nasal members, we got into one of the several four horse stage coaches of the "National Road and Good Intent Stage Company," whereby we were to be transported over those big hills. They did the thing systematically, whatever may be said elsewise. All the passengers' names were inscribed on a roll, (we purchased tickets in Philadelphia, at $13 a head, to go through to Wheeling,) and a clerk stands by and two or three negroes with a patent weighing machine. The clerk calls out your name—your baggage is whipped on the machine, and if it weighs over fifty pounds, you have to pay extra. You are then put in the stage, (literally put in, like a package, unless you move quickly,) your baggage packed on behind—the next name called off—baggage weighed—and so on to the end of the chapter. If six passengers desire it, or any smaller number who will pay for six, they can wait and have a coach sent, with them the next morning, or at any hour they choose. One cunning trick of the company is, that they give you no check or receipt for your baggage, for which they pretend to be not responsible. It is best therefore, if possible, for each passenger to have some witness to his baggage and its amount, in which case, if it be lost, the company will have to pay up—whatever they publish to the contrary.

So they boxed us up in our coach, nine precious souls, and we dashed through the town and up the mountains, with an apparent prospect of as comfortable a night as could be expected, considering all things. One or two of the passengers tried to get up a conversational entertainment; one old gentleman, in particular, *did* talk. He resided on a farm in the interior of Ohio. He had been on to Washington, (I heard the fact at least twenty-five times in the course of that night and the next day,) to claim a certain $5000 from the Government for capturing a British merchant brig, off the coast of Maine, in the last war. She got becalmed, or something of that sort, and he being thereabout, in command of a fishing smack, sailed or rowed up, captured her and brought her into port, where the Government functionaries took possession of her and sold her cargo for some $30,000. Our old gentleman, however, (not *then* old, of course,) had no privateering papers, and consequently was not a dollar the gainer. He had now been on to Washington to see about it, and was in hopes of getting at least his share of the sale. (Poor old man! if he lives till he gets Congress to pay him, he will be immortal.) This famous old gentleman moreover informed us that his wife had thirteen children, one in every month of the year, and one over besides—all being alive and kicking! He did not exactly know what to think about the Mexican war; but he thought that Congress might at least grant decent pensions to those who were severely maimed in it, and to the widows of both officers and privates who were killed. Sage and sound conclusions, thought the rest of us too. And here I may say, once for all, that, though expecting to find a shrewd population as I journeyed to the interior, and down through the great rivers, I was by no means prepared for the sterling vein of common sense that seemed to pervade them—even the roughest shod and roughest clad of all. A satirical person could no doubt find an ample field for his powers in many of the manners and ways of the West; and so can he, indeed, in the highest circle of fashion. But I fully believe that in a comparison of actual manliness and what the Yankees call "gumption," the well-to-do *citizens* (for I am not speaking so much of the country,) particularly the young men, of New York, Philadelphia, Boston, Brooklyn and so on, with all the advantages of compact neighborhood, schools, etc., are not up to the men of the West. Among the latter, probably, attention is more turned to the *realities* of life, and a habit formed of thinking for one's self; in the cities; frippery and artificial fashion are too much the ruling powers.

Up we toiled, and down we clattered, (for the first fifty miles it was nearly *all* up,) over these mighty warts on the great breast of nature. It was excessively cold; the moon shone at intervals; and whenever we stopped, I found the ground thickly covered with snow. The places at which we changed horses, (which was done every ten miles,) were generally long, old, one-story houses, with stupendous fires of the soft coal that is so plentiful and cheap here. In the night, with the mountains on all sides, the precipitous and turning road, the large, bare-armed trees looming up around us, the room half filled with men curiously enwrapped in garments of a fashion till then never seen—and the flickering light from the mighty fire putting a red glow upon most objects, and casting others into a strong shadow—I can tell you these stoppages were not without interest. They might, it seems to me, afford first rate scenes for an *American* painter—one who, not continually straining to be merely second or third best, in *imitation,* seizes original and really picturesque occasions of this sort for his pieces. There was one of the Alleghany inns, in particular, that we stopped at about an hour after midnight. (All the staging across these mountains, both to and fro, is done in the night, which engrafts a somewhat weird character upon the public houses—their busy time being from sunset to sunrise.) There were some ten or twelve great strapping drovers, reclining about the room on benches, and as many more before the huge fire. The beams overhead were low and smoke-dried. I stepped to the farther end of the long porch; the view from the door was grand, though vague, even in the moonlight. We had just descended a large and very steep hill, and just off on one side of us was a precipice apparently of hundreds of feet. The silence of the grave spread over this solemn scene; the mountains were covered in their white shrouds of snow—and the towering trees looked black and threatening; only the largest stars were visible, and they glittered with a ten-fold brightness. One's heart, at such times, is irresistibly lifted to Him of whom these august appearances are but the least emanation. Faith! if I had an infidel to convert, I would take him to the mountains, of a clear and beautiful night, when the stars are shining.

Journeying in this manner, the time and the distance slipped away, until we welcomed the gray dawn of the morning. Half an hour more brought us to Uniontown, at the western side of the Alleghanies—and glad enough were "all hands" to arrive there.

A Steamboat Bound for New Orleans.
From *Norman's New Orleans and Environs,* 1848.

———— ✦ ————

Cincinnati and Louisville
MONDAY, MARCH 6, 1848

It may well be doubted whether any large city in Christendom can show a more plentiful, or cheaper, supply of what are termed "provisions" than Cincinnati. All the richest and wholesomest products of the earth, pour in there, as into a sort of cornucopia—all that grows on the farms, or is rendered from the dairy, or the care of the poulterer. You can buy a pair of the fattest sort of chickens, in the markets there, for a quarter of a dollar, and many other things are in proportion. If it were possible, though, to make the side bank which rises up from the Ohio any thing else except the ungainly *mud* which it is nearly all the time, the city in question would be hugely the gainer among that large class "people in general." That miry bank gives any thing but an agreeable character to those who see Cincinnati from the river: it could certainly be remedied, and to the profit, too, of passengers, drays, and horses. A favorite name for the shops, as a prefix, is that of "Queen City." One may notice many a "Queen City Segar Store," and "Queen City Clothing Emporium," etc. The friendly invitation of "Walk In" is also inscribed on about one-third of the shop window lights. With New York and New Orleans, Cincinnati undoubtedly makes *the* trio of business places in this republic—though Philadelphia must not be forgotten either. There are very large and flourishing manufactories at Cincinnati, and the retail stores vie with those of the sea-board. If the advice be not considered impertinent, however, we should advise the city papers to have the streets cleaned, and kept so, "regardless of expense."

Louisville, one hundred and fifty miles further down on the Ohio, is a smaller and considerably quieter city than the one above named. It has a *substantial* look to him who walks through it for the first time; and, withal, does not a little business in provisions, too. Most of the boats passing on the Ohio rendezvous here—and if it were not for the ugly "falls" just below the city, (avoided by a canal on the Kentucky side,) doubtless there would be still more from below. Louisville has many noble and hospitable citizens, whose family circles make a "happy time" for him who gets on visiting terms with them.

———— ✦ ————

Western Steamboats—The Ohio

FRIDAY, MARCH 10, 1848

H aving crossed the Alleghanies during Saturday night, and spent the ensuing day in weary stages, from Uniontown onward, we arrived at Wheeling a little after 10 o'clock on Sunday night, and went on board the steamer St. Cloud, a freight and packet boat, lying at the wharf there, with the steam all up, and ultimately bound for New Orleans. This was my "first appearance" on a Western steamboat. The long cabin, neatly carpeted, and lit with clusters of handsome lamps, had no uncomfortable look; but the best comfort of the mat-

ter lay in (what I myself soon laid in) a good state room, of which I took possession, and forthwith was oblivious to all matters of a waking character. Roused
next morning by the clang of the breakfast bell, I found that we had during the
night made a good portion of our way toward Cincinnati.

Like as in many other matters, people who travel on the Ohio, (that most
beautiful of words!) for the first time, will stand a chance of being somewhat
disappointed. In poetry and romance, these rivers are talked of as though they
were cleanly streams; but it is astonishing what a difference is made by the simple fact that they are always and altogether excessively muddy—mud, indeed,
being the prevailing character both afloat and ashore. This, when one thinks
of it, is not only reasonable enough, but unavoidable in the very circumstances
of the case. Yet, it destroys at once the principal beauty of the rivers. There
is no romance in a mass of yellowish brown liquid. It is marvellous, though,
how easily a traveller gets to drinking it and washing in it. What an india-
rubber principle, there is, after all, in humanity!

To one who beholds steamboat-life on the Ohio for the first time, there
will of course be many fresh features and notable transpirings. One of the first,
and most unpleasant, is the want of punctuality in departing from places, and
consequently the same want in arriving at them. All the steamers carry freight,
that being, indeed, their principal business and source of profit, to which the
accommodation of passengers, (as far as this is concerned) has to stand sec-
ondary. We on the St. Cloud, for instance, picked up all sorts of goods from all
sorts of places, wherever our clever little captain made a bargain for the same.
What he brought down from Pittsburg, the Lord only knows; for we took in
afterward what would have been considered a very fair cargo to a New York
liner. At one place, for instance, we shipped several hundred barrels of pork;
ditto of lard; at another place, an uncounted (by me) lot of flour—enough,
though, it seemed, to have fed half the office-holders of the land—and that is
saying something. Besides these, we had bags of coffee, rolls, of leather, groce-
ies, dry goods, hardware, all sorts of agricultural products, innumerable coops
filled with live geese, turkeys, and fowls, that kept up a perpetual farm-yard
concert. Then there were diverse living hogs, to say nothing of a horse, and
a resident dog. The country through which the Ohio runs is one of the most
productive countries—and one of the most buying and selling—in the world;

and nearly all the transportation is done on steamboats. Putting those two facts together, one can get an idea of the infinite variety, as well as amount, of our cargo. To my eyes it was enormous; though people more used to such things didn't seem to consider it any wonder at all.

About half past 6 o'clock, on board those boats—I begin at the beginning, you see—the breakfast bell is rung, giving the passengers half an hour to prepare for the table. Of edibles, for breakfast, (as at the other meals, too,) the quantity is enormous, and the quality first rate. The difference is very wide between the table here and any public table at the north-east; the latter, as many a starved wight can bear testimony, being in most cases, arranged on a far more economical plan. The worst of it is, on the Western steamboats, that every body gulps down the victuals with railroad speed. With that distressing want of a pleasant means to pass away time, which all travellers must have experienced, is it not rather astonishing that the steamboat breakfast or dinner has to be dispatched in five minutes?

During the day, passengers amuse themselves in various ways. Cheap novels are in great demand, and a late newspaper is a gem almost beyond price. From time to time, the boat stops, either for wood or freight; sometimes to pick up a passenger who hails from the shore. At the stopping places on the Kentucky side, appear an immense number of idlers, boys, old farmers, and tall, strapping, comely young men. At the stopping places on the Northern shore, there seems to be more thrift and activity. The shore, each way, is much of it barren of interest; though the period must arrive when cultivation will bend it nearly all to man's use. Here and there, already, is a comfortable house; and, at intervals, there are tracts of well-tilled land, particularly on the Ohio line.

In the evening, (the reader must remember that it is not for *one* evening only, but sometimes for ten or twelve,) the passenger spends his time according to fancy. In our boat, the St. Cloud, the two large cabin tables were sometimes surrounded by readers; and the stove by smokers and talkers. The ladies appeared to have rather a dull time of it in their place. Most of them would sit listlessly for hours doing nothing—and, so far as I could learn, saying nothing!

Among the principal incidents of the voyage was crossing the falls of the Ohio, just below Louisville. Our boat was very deeply laden; and though there is a canal around the ticklish pass; our captain, with Western hardihood, determined to go over the "boiling place." For my own part, I didn't know till afterwards, but that it was an every hour occurrence. The bottom of the boat grated harshly more than once on the stones beneath, and the pilots showed plainly that they did not feel altogether as calm as a summer morning. We passed over, however, in perfect safety. The Ohio here has a fall of many feet in the course of a mile. Does not the perfection to which engineering has been brought afford some means of remedying this ugly part of the river? Besides the canal around on the Kentucky side, the Indiana Legislature has lately granted a charter for one on its shore, too.

From Louisville down, one passes through a long stretch of monotonous country—not varied at all, sometimes for dozens of miles. The Ohio retains its distinctive character of mud, till you get to the very end of it.

Cairo, at the junction of the Mississippi, pointed our passage into the great Father of Waters. Immense sums of money have been spent to make Cairo something like what a place with such a name ought to be. But with the exception of its position, which is unrivalled for business purposes, every thing about it seems unfortunate. The point on which it is situated, is low, and liable to be overflowed at every high flood. Besides, it is unwholesomely wet, at the best. It is doubtful whether Cairo will ever be any "great shakes," except in the way of ague.

The Mouth of the Mississippi.
From *Norman's New Orleans and Environs,* 1848.

———— ✦ ————

The Mississippi at Midnight

MONDAY, MARCH 6, 1848

How solemn! sweeping this dense black tide!
No friendly lights i' the heaven o'er us;
A murky darkness on either side,
And kindred darkness all before us!
Now, drawn nearer, the shelving rim,
Weird-like shadows suddenly rise;
Shapes of mist and phantoms dim
Baffle the gazer's straining eyes.
River fiends, with malignant faces!
Wild and wide their arms are thrown,
As if to clutch in fatal embraces
Him who sails their realms upon.
Then, by the trick of our swift motion,
Straight, tall giants, an army vast,
Rank by rank, like the waves of ocean,
On the shore march stiffly past,
How solemn! the river a trailing pall,
Which takes, but never again gives back;
And moonless and starless the heaven's arch'd wall,
Responding an equal black!
Oh, tireless waters! like Life's quick dream,
Onward and onward ever hurrying—
Like Death in this midnight hour you seem,
Life in your chill drops greedily burying!

SKETCHES of NEW ORLEANS

REPORTER'S MOTTO.—By these presents be it known, that the Reporters for the daily newspapers of the city of New Orleans have, for a long time, desired a motto to be placed upon their coat of arms, etc. etc. As they have to *walk some,* we respectfully suggest that they adopt the Latin quotation of "*Necessitas non habet LEG-em.*"

—*New Orleans Daily Crescent,* May 11, 1848

———— ✦ ————

Novelties in New Orleans

MONDAY, MARCH 13, 1848

We have frequently heard foreigners say that "New Orleans was a very beautiful place, but that, dem it, it had no places of amusement." We throw back the remark, with the most excellent good humor, into their very teeth, and sincerely hope that, they may never have any thing worse than the best tooth-brush that can be procured to clean their masticators with. New Orleans without places of amusement! Why the very idea, gentlemen, is absolutely absurd. If there be any individual in the community who has Santa Anna's favorite passion on the apex of his heart—which remark meaneth a furious desire to be present when the Gallic emblem of nationality spurs himself for the fight—he can at all times be accommodated in the lower municipalities. In certain locations he will be permitted to cry—"Crow, Chapman—Chapman, crow!" to the fullest extent of his lungs. Does the gentleman desire to see an Attakapas bull (just imported from Havana) speared by an artiste of celebrity? If so, his wish can be fulfilled by visiting Algiers and the Third Municipality, in the pleasant season of our Southern summer. As for masquerade

Bird's Eye View of New Orleans, ca. 1850, by John Bachman (detail).
Library of Congress.

Balls, we can only be beaten by gay, gallant, chivalrous Paris: and in the way of operas, we can't be beaten at all. There's the French opera at the Orleans Theatre, with its magnificent troupe; and occasionally we have those addicted to music from the "Father-land," who sing to our uneducated ears, strains of the most mysterious sweetness.—Again, once or twice in the course of the theatrical season, we have gems of genius in the way of vocalists from the "sunny skies of fair, classic Italy," who sing as if their very blood had been intermixed with the red currents that flow through the hearts of nightingales. Therefore, as Bombastes says—

"Since Music is the fool of love,
Play Michael Wiggins once again!"

If a person wishes to perforate his intimate friend or insolent enemy, he has only to go to some one of the numerous shooting-galleries in New Orleans, and by the joint aid of a few dimes and three days' practice, he can be taught to split a bullet against the edge of a pen-knife, at the distance of ten paces. Those, too, who are fond of playing with edged tools, will, by applying to some of our fencing-masters, be taught how to "pink" a gentleman in a manner that Chevalier Bayard would have wept at. More than this could not be desired.

Now, as for our National Drama, we have all the materials necessary. Stars from Europe, from Britain, and, aye, sometimes from our own wild Western States, appear week after week at the different Theatres—which "temples of the drama" are, we suppose, better patronized than any others in "the land of the free and the home of the brave." Those who come to visit us, albeit for a season, must never think that the Queen City of the South is deficient in amusements—for they can enjoy themselves at any thing in the way of drinking, from a glass of the waters of the muddy Mississippi, up to a golden goblet filled with Roman punch:—in the way of eating, from a mouldy sea-biscuit with a slice of rusty bacon, up to broiled, pompano with terrapin eggs and asparagus; and in the way of music, from the tooting of a penny whistle, up to a soul-entrancing strain of a silver bugle, in the still, solemn hours of night.

The fact is, that in this goodly city, we can go through the whole alphabet of enjoyment, and, as they say in the West, "not miss a letter from A to Izzard."

———— + ————

Firemen Celebration

SUNDAY, MARCH 5, 1848

The Annual Celebration of the Firemen of New Orleans took place yesterday, and although the commencement of the morning gave token of
murky weather, still the indication did not dissuade them from turning out in
full numbers. The sky was the color of lead, and the streets were ankle deep in
mud—the air seemed to come from an ice house; but even as summer drives
winter away, the streams of music from the different bands drove every cold,
melancholy thought from the hearts of those who viewed the brilliant procession. Shortly after the appointed hour, the gallant concourse formed in line,
and proceeded according to the programme through the principal streets. The
procession was followed by the glance of the brilliant eye of beauty, and the ac-
clamations of brave and gallant men. The engines were decked with flowers—
the firemen were clad in their gayest suits, and every emblem gave token that
it was a day of rejoicing to the philanthropic and the brave.

Oh, how proud it made one feel of this country, to see those stalwart men
leading along the engines of peace, not of destruction—engines destined not
to batter down the walls, but to preserve the threshold and the household
gods of those who were their brothers! Their motto, like that of the ancient
chivalry, was "Ready—aye—ready!" At glimmering morn, mid-day sun, grey
evening, or gloomy midnight—aye, even when the rain hurtled against the
shivering casement, and the lightning flashed—these brave men had been at
their post. No danger could intimidate them—no struggle could bear down
the strength of the firemen of New Orleans. Like brothers, at the first stroke
of the alarm bell, they rush to their quarters—drag forth with almost super-
natural strength their engines, and when they saved the lives of hundreds, and
the property may be of thousands, peacefully retire to their homes.

Yesterday was the anniversary of the gallant firemen of New Orleans. The
banner of the stripes and stars was waving in every street, and at every corner
strains of music that stirred the soul were heard. At the appointed hour, the
procession passed up and down the principal streets and the members were

the "observed of all observers." Shouts of applause rent the air as the splendid procession passed along; and as though Heaven had deigned to look smilingly upon the celebration, not an accident occurred to mar the festivities of the day. All was cheerfulness, joy and happiness, and our gallant firemen knew that they deserved and appreciated the compliments and congratulations that were yesterday so gladly lavished upon them.

At a few minutes before 3 o'clock the different companies entered the American Theatre, and after they had been seated the orator of the day, George W. Harby, Esq., delivered a most beautiful and impressive address. In a feeling and philanthropic tone he spoke of the duties of the fireman, and compared him not to the one who went forth to destroy, but to him who "girded his loins to save." The remarks of the talented orator drew down bursts of applause, and we much regret that our columns will not allow us to give his oration in full. Suffice it to say, the address of Mr. Harby was marked by the imprint of genius, and certainly more than fulfilled the expectations of those who had chosen him as the orator of the day.

When the oration had been concluded, a select part of the firemen repaired to the Commercial Exchange, kept by Messrs. Clark & Hickok, where they were served with a splendid collation. Here the "red wine freely flowed," and that gentle spirit peace, accompanied by her generous though somewhat boisterous brother, hilarity, as the old poem sayeth—

"Blessed the beeves, aye an the kine
Of all sorts—and the dulcet wine!"

———— ✦ ————

The Sabbath
MONDAY, MARCH 6, 1848

Yesterday was a beautiful day—such a day as Wordsworth would have loved—and albeit, we have neither the silver Tweed nor the green-fringed Clyde to glide upon, still we had scenes that made us marvel at the beneficence of our Maker. The gigantic Mississippi, bearing on her broad bosom many a royal argossie—the densely populated town, where man was at peace with his fellow-man, and where love and charity prevailed, and the forests of tall green trees that surrounded our prosperous city, all attested the kindness of the Ruler above. Business, for the most part, was suspended, and many there were who walked forth to contemplate the natural beauties which environed the "proud city of the South." The living streams of human beings that flowed from the different houses of worship, showed that our citizens were not wanting in godliness, and the peace that prevailed proved that we dwelt together, as Scripture beautifully expresses it, "a loving community." Those silent abodes of the dead, were not without their visiters. Many a tear was dropped upon the white tomb-stone covering the form of him who was dear in life, and who was not forgotten even though "dust had been given unto dust." The heart of the mother wailed when she saw the tiny grave of her first born, and many a manly breast heaved with that emotion which sorrow only knows, when the pale ornaments built over the departed, came in view. Still, with all the cares and perplexities of life, Hope, the harbinger of happiness, loomed high in the horizon of the future, and every face we met with in the busy thoroughfares, and highways of this great city, seemed redolent with joy. Yesterday was the Sabbath of the calendar. Heaven grant it may have been the "Sabbath of the heart" to all.

———— ✦ ————

Daguerreotype Portraits
MONDAY, MARCH 6, 1848

S hade of Daguerre, we invoke thee! Thy pencil was composed of sunbeams, and thy palette was colored o'er only by golden tints. Thou had'st not the cerulean, the beautiful blue symbol of Hope—the signal so full of joy to the mariner, who, when in the desert of a stormy ocean, looks up to Heaven for relief and succor! Thou had'st not the purple—that color which tinges, and makes apparent royalty of birth or accident; nor the red, which speaks to us in a sword-like tongue, and spirits forth narrow streams of blood. And last, buy *aye*, not least, though did'st not have the yellow—that loathsome color, the emblem of hate, anger, and revenge! Thy magnificent genius taught thee, oh Daguerre! to take down the semblance of men, women and children, on thin sheets of metal, plated with thinner sheets of silver—but oh! how much brass we frequently see in their countenances. Daguerre, stepson of Phœbus, again we invoke thee! See some of the specimens of the work which thou has't wrought:

Mrs. Jinkins.—Mr. Doggertipe, I want me and my baby takin. You needn't say nothin about the child's shoes and pantaletts, but merely do it as the picture—people say, at half length, leavin off the baby's legs and her stockins. As for me, I want you to take me as I am, with my child upon my knee, and my right hand claspin her around the waist. I want a sweet kind of smile, painted on my features, and to have the baby danglin with its left hand in my hair.

Mr. See-Island (a cotton broker.)—Sir: I wish you to paint me in the attitude of the merchant in profound speculation—with one hand in my bosom and the other negligently supporting my massive forehead. And, Sir, be particularly careful of the cornelian watch-seal—it was a gift from my father, Sir, a merchant in the Liverpool trade, and I would not part with it for the world.

Hon. John Jones.—How do you do, sir! I wish to have my likeness taken immediately. The fact is, (nobody is here, is there?) the President has sent for *me,* upon what business, however, I know not, but as I *may* be sent to Mexico, I would like my family to have some memento—you understand. [Here the Hon. John Jones hid his face behind his hat, for he was overcome with emotion.] Paint me with a large blue cloak hanging over my left shoulder, my eyes looking to the Capitol, and if you can get it in, stick a gold-headed cane in my hand.

Miss Snibbs.—(This lady has on a remarkably small bonnet, and a bewitching smile.) What do you charge, sir? Can you take me with gloves on, sir? Certainly, Miss Snibbs seats herself upon a chair and undergoes the solar operation.

Jack Tompkins.—Look here, old feller, how long will it take you to fetch me down. I sell horses and sometimes play cards. I want you to put me down by a table—stick a decanter by my side, and let Bowse, my big dog, put his nose between my legs. Git down, you cussed dog! don't you know you are goin' to have your'e portrate takin'?"

Albert Allbright.—"My deer sir, I wish you to take my daguerreotype." "How would you like to sit, sir?" "Oh, almost any way—but I would prefer that you would take me with a small centre-table by my side, together with a few champagne glasses, and some dominoes, and by the bye, a few promiscuous cards would not be amiss. But above all things, sir, put a cigar in my mouth and make the smoke as curly as possible!"

Oh golden shadow—thou bright phantom of art—thou sun-born child, "can such things be, and overcome us like a summer's cloud!" Only think that the God of Day condescends to paint in his own radiant colors the lineaments of Mrs. Jinkins!

———— ✦ ————

"The Season," Hereabouts

TUESDAY, MARCH 7, 1848

O ur Northern friends would be not a little surprised to witness the appearance of things, in the vegetable world, that characterizes the neighborhood of our "Crescent City," about these times. For some two weeks past we have been more and more surrounded by sights of spring—the green leaves, the blossoming of early trees, and so on. At the period of this present writing, vegetation hereabouts is as far advanced as it is in the latitude of New York by May, or the latter part of April. The beautiful green of our orange trees strikes the stranger always with a pleasant feeling—and particularly when he sees them growing, now, in full verdure in the open grounds.

It is a great pity that the planting of shade trees, in some of our public places, as in Lafayette Square and Canal street, does not succeed altogether well. Is this unavoidably the case? Surely perseverance and care will overcome the difficulty. Nothing could be pleasanter or more grateful, during the hot season in our city, than the refreshing presence of numerous large shade trees through our streets, and, indeed all about the city.

We find some remarks in the South Carolinian newspaper, which will not be amiss for this latitude, too, on the subject of shrubbery and shade trees, as follows:

Shade trees are indispensable in our climate, around and in front of our dwellings. In the first settlement of our country, trees were looked upon as the natural enemies of the soil, and they were cut down without mercy; in many in-stances not a single tree was suffered to remain near the dwelling. A better feeling in their favor begins to infuse itself, and in many cases among our improving planters forest trees may be seen planted and grown around their homesteads. Some efforts, too, are beginning to be made to have the different choice varieties of fruits added to their orchards, and ornamental shrubs and trees are to be found around the homestead, while the honeysuckle, the climb-ing rose, and Carolina's favorite jessamine neatly trimmed, give to the place an air of beauty and comfort. How desolate and uninviting does even a good home look, without the little ornaments which a tasteful hand might throw around it, at a trifling cost!

The ladies, who possess an inherent love for neatness and beauty, must insist upon the embellishment of the exterior as well as the interior of their dwellings.

When we see a neglected garden, and a bare yard without a shrub or flower to beautify it, we are half inclined to blame the ladies who reside there; for their influence generally prevails; and why should it not in this respect, if properly exercised? We look to their aid in carrying out these improvements, and in some instances we know we shall not look in vain.

We hope truly that a spirit of encouragement to the growth of those chil-dren of the soil, flowers and shrubbery and trees, will not be always kept down in our city, by the engrossing business cares of so many of our citizens. We are convinced that the developed of this sprit could much beautify and benefit the place, and make it more a place of *homes*.

———— ✦ ————

Mardi Gras

WEDNESDAY, MARCH 8, 1848

Yesterday was the famous day for those who wished to see the colors of the rainbow in streets and squares. All the principal avenues were filled with persons dressed in the most grotesque costumes. The "turbaned Moor"

Mardi Gras in 1867. If Whitman's hotel was still extant at the time, it would be visible
on the third block up the road from the St. Charles Hotel in the direction
of the parade, close to the flags displayed in the center left.
From *Frank Leslie's Illustrated,* 1867.

had his face indelibly made lily white by a dash of flour thrown by the hand
of some inelegant imp who had less brains than wit. By-the-bye, we were glad
to see that several of this tribe of promiscuous and uncompromising rascals
got what "Paddy gave the drum," yesterday, for various acts of impertinence.
The celebration of "Mardi Gras" is very pretty, but throwing flour in the face
of a man whose imagination is not flowery is an unpoetic act, and moreover,
a diabolical abomination. No accidents, however, thanks be to Providence,
occurred. Those females who personated the amazon, bestrode their horses,
with all the gracefulness of Joan d'Arc. They looked "considerable" in their purple velvet pantaloons and Turkish pantalets. King Otho, of Greece, the gentleman who used to "snack it" with Lord Byron, would have enjoyed the scene
amazingly. The masculine department of this time-honored celebration, was
well attended, and the brave and loyal may repose themselves upon the green
laurels which they gained yesterday. To say that a nervous young lady, or a

hysterical old grandmamma, would not have been frightened into fits at the sight of the hideous masques, worn by those who "cavorted" about yesterday, would subject any "penny-a-liner" to the workhouse, or, strictly speaking, a more comfortable place—Baton Rouge. But as Dickson of York once said, let's "Take to something of more serious method"—Mardi Gras was celebrated yesterday in a very handsome manner, and, upon our conscience, we do not believe that more than a dozen fights took place during the day.

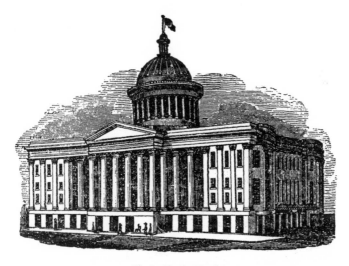

The St. Charles Hotel.
From *Norman's New Orleans and Environs,* 1848.

---- ✦ ----

The Habitants of Hotels

FRIDAY, MARCH 10, 1848

There is no actual need of a man's travelling around the globe in order to find out a few of the principles of human nature. The observer needn't even go to a college or a primary school, but if he is determined to supply himself with knowledge, let him visit the precincts of some of our "first-rate, tip-top" bar-rooms on Saturday or Sunday night.

That young gentleman, with the shiney black coat and the unexceptionable pantaloons, is the very pink of propriety. He is very particular about the quality of the crape that he wears upon his hat, and is excessively fond of mild Havana segars. He invariably uses a tooth-brush with an ivory handle, and is partial to watering-places in the summer-time, and gambling houses when the "Norwegian season" takes place. A large diamond breast-pin, and a massive gold chain attached to a galvanized watch, are generally his ornaments. The cock-pit for him is a favorite place of resort, and he occasionally "splurges" himself at a game of cards. When the yellow fever season commences, the gentleman in question darts like an arrow northward, and spends his summer at Saratoga or Niagara Falls.

Now yonder is an elderly gentleman, who seems to desire to bite the head off a gold-mounted cane. By way of varying his mode of enjoyment, he occasionally twirls his watch-seal and about twice in every half hour motions the bar-keeper to mix him a brandy toddy. Gentlemen of this class generally live in the West, in South America, or Mexico. This description of gentlemen are generally adepts in all matters pertaining to horse-flesh, and in the selection of Bowie knives and shooting galleries, are philosophers "beyond compare." Their conversational powers are generally devoted to descriptions of duels, awful, conflicts by sea and land, and stories of how bluff old Major So-and-So gave a terrible flogging to Col. This-and-That more than twenty years ago.

How gracefully he leans back in his chair, and what a "Count D'Orsay" fling there is to his to his blue broadcloth cloak! How beautifully the gold spectacles set upon his pallid proboscis!—and his teeth—why, bless us! they glisten like pearls. See, he inserts a silver tooth-pick between the interstices of his ivories, and smiles as though he felt extremely happy. What can he be thinking of? A theory on the principle of gravitation—some beautiful idea collated from the philosophy of Emanuel Swedenborg, or the price of putty? Of neither—he is thinking of nothing but the extraction of corns, of Mesmerism, and the consequences of chloroform. The gentleman alluded to will make money, buy a big seal ring, cultivate an imperial, go to Europe, get dubbed a Professor of almost any thing in the way of Science or Art, bring a troupe of "Model Artists" across the Atlantic, and become the "lion of the day."

That young man with the bandy legs, who is standing with his back to the stove, has just arrived from New York. He prides himself upon the neatness of the tie of his crimson neckcloth, and professes to be a connoisseur in everything relating to pea-nuts. Whilst he puffs the smoke of a remarkably bad segar directly underneath your nostrils, he will discourse most learnedly about the classical performances in the Chatham Theatre, and swear by some heathen god or goddess that "Kirby was one of 'em, and no mistake." This is one of the "b'hoys of the Bowery." He strenuously contends that Mr. N. P. Willis is a humbug—that Mike Walsh is a "hoss," and that the Brigadier "ain't no where." The great probability is that the "b'hoy" in question never saw either of the gentlemen that he attempts to lampoon. The vista of his imagination certainly does not extend beyond Baton Rouge.

A hickory stick and a hickory soul—both are stern and stalwart—both are firm and honest. Commend us to the old grey-haired farmer, whose withered fingers grasp with an iron clutch his trusty cane! Who would believe it? That old man is the father of a Senator! He subscribes for the "Union" and "National Intelligencer," and many a times his eyes are brightened with the "silver tears of joy," when he hears the name of his first-born mentioned. The cultivation of potatoes and turnips—the thrashing of the little stock of wheat, and the sale of the little field of corn, brought money to send the son to college. Intense energy, application to study, determination and industry made the farmer's son a shining light amongst his fellows. The good old farmer! His son discusses questions of the greatest importance at Washington—tells Robert Peel and John Russell that they are entirely wrong—cautions Louis Philippe against some European policy, and requests Prince Metternich to be upon his guard lest he should fail in his diplomatic conclusions! Turnips and talent—potatoes and politics—"pumpkins" (some) and professions!

The parlor of the hotel we will not enter, but when we have a pen, virgin so far as ink is concerned—any quantity of satin paper with gilded edges, and a few gallons of cologne, who shall endeavor to describe the peculiarities of those chosen mortals who will live above board—or, at least above the bar-room.

+ + +

A Sabbath Pastime: New Orleans Cock-Fighting.
From *Every Saturday*, 1871.

———— ✦ ————

Sketches of the Sidewalks and Levee;
With Glimpses into the New Orleans Bar (rooms)

Peter Funk, Esq.

MONDAY, MARCH 13, 1848

To illustrate the "life, fortune and sacred honor" of the distinguished individual whose name leads off our present sketch of noted characters, is a task as tasteful as it is agreeable. The duty of the faithful chronologist and biographer is particularly a cheerful one when the subject of such notice is calculated to heighten the interest we feel in the dignity and delicate sensibilities of human nature.

Funk, like all other illustrious personages who have become so well known as no longer to need the titular soubriquet of *Mister,* was born and brought up—no one knows where: at least the information we have on this point is exceedingly uncertain and contradictory. Without, therefore, descending into the particulars of his early training and history, or minutely tracing up the rationale of cause and effect, by showing that a youth of moral proclivity will, in time, run into that species of moral gum-elasticity which goes to constitute the blood and bones of individuals comprising his *genus,* we shall proceed at once, *in medias res,* as the boys say at college, and make known to you, gentle reader, that Peter Funk is a young gentleman "about town" who holds the highly responsible office of by-bidder in a Mock Auction—being engaged to said work by "the man wot sells the watches."

You're a gentleman of leisure about Orleans, may be, stranger, and lounging about —— street. You hear the musical sound of the "human voice divine," crying out "fivenaff, five-n-a-ff—only going at twenty-five dollars and-n-a-ff for this elegant gold watch and chain, in prime running order, just sent in to be sold by a *gentleman leaving town,* and only five-n-a-ff, and must be sold: five-n-a-ff! Did I hear you say six, sir?" Perhaps you drop in, and if you are not careful how you look at the musical auctioneer he will accept of your look for a wink, and, according to the philosophy of the auction room, a wink passes for a bid, and you find yourself in nominal possession of "an elegant gold watch and chain, in prime running order, just sent in to be sold by a gentleman leav-

A Shady Peter Funk.
From *New York in Slices,* 1848.

ing town," before you are well aware of what you are about. So take care how you look when you are in the patent auction shops. There stands the auctioneer in all the serious earnestness of a man begging for his life, and, with voice and looks and gestures, seems like one speaking sober truth, and "nothin' else." Only half a dozen individuals comprise his audience, and these half a dozen are Peter Funk and his *corps de reserve.* Peter looks somewhat stouter to-day than he was yesterday, and has exchanged his cloth cloak and cap for a blanket coat and *chapeau blanc,* and his whiskers have shared the fate of "the last rose of summer"—that is to say, they have evaporated—dropped off: they are *non est inventus*—gone.

Yes, that's Funk and his five interesting associates in business—"companions of his toil, his feelings and his fame"—Peter the 1st, Peter the 2d, Peter the 3d, Peter the 4th and Peter the 5th—he himself being no other than Peter the Great, or the greater Peter—"Peter Funk, Esq."

Now, stranger, take care what you're about—you're the only bona fide customer—if customer you choose to call yourself—that has entered the portals of the auction shop as yet, and Peter Funk Primus and Peter Funk Secundus have done all this bidding that makes the cryer keep up such a hubbaboo. Well, you do n't know of this fact, and you think "A man's a man for a' that," and you don't understand the secret of Peter Funk and his associates, or the service they're engaged in, and you only see a fine-*looking* watch, "just sent in to be sold by a gentleman leaving town," and going dog cheap. You nod your head, and straitway the countenance of the cryer brightens up, and his voice grows even more vociferous than before. He's got a bid—a real bid—and the first and only one. He tack no five dollars more, and now he's heard going it in fine style: "Thirty, thirty, thirty, thirty, thirty—only going at thirty dollars for a splendid elegant gold lever, with seventeen pairs of extra jewels, lately imported, and now must be sold!"

He cries on at this rate for perhaps ten minutes, occasionally casting a glance at the passers-by to see if any more *greeneys* can be tolled in. Peter Funk takes the watch in his hand and examines it attentively, and with a very significant look, as though his judgement was perfectly satisfied, he says deliberately, "Thirty-five!"

"Against you, sir," cries Mr. Auctioneer, and forthwith sets off with unusual volubility, crying out one *rotundo,* "thirty-five, thirty-five—only going at thirty-five!"

Thirty-five dollars for such an elegant gold watch is certainly as cheap as dirt—they ask eighty-five or ninety at the stores:—and as these thoughts revolve in your mind, you think you might make five and twenty dollars as well as not, as there are plenty of boys up in your country who would jump at the bargain—and you not again, the auctioneer having in the meanwhile directed the whole force of his vocable artillery at you, and launched forth in such a rigmarole of praise of said time-piece, that you could n't well resist his very passionate appeal.

"Forty dollars!" is quickly caught up. "Only going at forty dollars!—forty! forty! forty! forty!" and now the cryer turns to Peter, the interesting Peter, whose turn for *serious deliberation* has again come. He again examines the watch, turns it over and over again, and, as he hands it to the cryer, says in a very low but decided tone of voice, "forty-five!"

By this time one or two other loungers like yourself have dropped in, and monsieur cryer applies himself with exceeding earnestness in lauding the watch, as never, sure, watch was lauded before, except perhaps at a patent auction.

While you are revolving in your mind whether "to go" the *fifty,* some other greeney from one of the upper parishes, or may be from Mississippi, with his pockets full of money, cries out "fifty, by G—d! " and you are relieved from what would have been a very dear bargain to you—the invoice of said "elegant gold lever" having been only $17 50! Like Hodge's razors, they are "made to sell," and many are the green 'uns that are bit, awfully bit, by the "persuasive speech" of the auctioneer, and still more persuasive biddings of his interesting coadjutor in this pretty business, Peter Funk, Esq., the subject of our present "sketch."

I was pretty well acquainted with Funk before he went into the "Auction and Commission business"; we boarded a while together at the same house. Since his embarkation into the business of *buying watches,* we have grown offish with one another: he never knows me in the auction room, though we may be standing side by side; and, to the various disguises he assumes, for he scarcely ever dresses the same for two days in succession—being in cap, cloak and whiskers on one day, and the next *aliased* up in a white or green blanket. Some say he was from Old Kentuck, and others again aver he is a North Carolina Tennesseean while "other some" allege him to have been a direct importation from the nethermost corner of Down East—having resided a year or two in Texas by way of a seasoning—and that he is an "own cousin" of the "rat man," and also of kin to him "wot cleans coat collars." Of this I can say nothing—but am of opinion that if even Peter Funk received a "fotching up" according to old-fashioned New England Puritanism, he must have become amazingly warped in his morals ere he reached the latitude of Louisiana.

To sum up the character I have to give of Peter Funk, I shall simply say, that he at present thrives well, and will make a business man of himself if he keeps on. He is one of those men who reverse the saying of Hamlet, that "conscience make cowards of us all." Peter's conscience makes no coward of him—*argal,* Peter'll be rich one of these days. It's a bad thing to have

—"The native hue of resolution
Thus sicklied o'er with the pale cast of thought";

and Peter takes none of these sickly thoughts, or any other consideration, "for the morrow," except it be what coat, or what colored whiskers he shall put on.

———— ✦ ————

Sketches of the Sidewalks and Levee; With Glimpses into the New Orleans Bar (rooms)

Miss Dusky Grisette

THURSDAY, MARCH 16, 1848

Miss Dusky Grisette is the young "lady" who takes her stand of evening upon the pavement opposite the St. Charles Hotel, for the praiseworthy purpose of selling a few flowers by retail, showing off her own charms meanwhile, in a wholesale manner. She drives a thriving trade when the evenings are pleasant. Her neat basket of choice bouquets sits by her side, and she has a smile and a wink for every one of the passers-by who have a wink and a smile for her.

Mademoiselle Grisette was "raised" in the city, and is pretty well known as a very pretty *marchande des fleurs.* She can recommend a tasteful bunch of posies with all the grace in the world, and her "buy a broom" style of addressing her acquaintances has, certainly, something very taking about it. She possesses pretty eyes, a pretty chin, and a mouth that many an heiress, grown oldish and faded, would give thousands for. The *em bon point* of her form is full of attraction, and she dresses with simple neatness and taste. She keeps her eyes open and her mouth shut, except it be to show her beautiful teeth—ah, her's are teeth that are teeth. She has sense enough to keep her tongue quiet, and discourses more by "silence that speaks and eloquence of eyes" than any other method—herein she is prudent.

Grisette is not "a blue" by any means, rather a *brune,* or more prettily, a *brunette*—"but that's not much"; the vermillion of her cheeks shows through the veil; and her long glossy hair is *nearly straight.* There are many who affect the *brune* rather than the *blonde,* at least when they wish to purchase a bouquet— and as

—"Night
Shows stars and women in a better light,"

they leave a pleasant smile and a bewitching glance thrown into the bargain whilst purchasing a bunch of posies.

What becomes of the flower-girl in the day time, would be hard to tell: perhaps it would be in bad taste to attempt to find out. She is only interesting in character and association. Standing at, or reclining against, the door-cheeks of a store, with the brilliancy of the gas-light falling favorably, and perhaps deceptively, upon her features and upon her person, with her basket of tasteful bouquets at her feet, and some of her choicest buds fancifully setting off her own head-dress. As such, she looks in character as a *jolie grisette,* as she is, and will excite the notice of those who, beneath the light of the sun, and in the

New Orleans Flower Girls.
From *Ballou's Pictorial,* 1855.

noontide gaze of men, would spurn and loathe such familiarities. Poor Grisette, therefore slinks away to some retired hole or corner when the witching hours of gas-light have passed by, and when the walkers upon the streets grow tired of wandering, and with noise, have thrown themselves upon their beds for repose. She sells her flowers, and barters off sweet looks for sweeter money; and with her empty basket upon her head, she takes up "the line of march" for her humble home, along with "daddy" who, being ever upon the safe look-out, has come after her.

Perhaps, in the morning, she sells coffee at one of the street corners, to the early draymen, who have an appetite for the regaling draught—becoming "all things to all men" in changing *tout a fait* her set of customers. In this last employment, she sylph-like puts on the air and manner of drudgery. Habited in a plain frock with a check apron, and with her head "bound about" by a cotton handkerchief, she retails bad coffee at a picayune a cup, with an air of *nonchalance* entirely suited to the calling and to the customers. Hard-working men like draymen, want coffee and not glances—they need the stomach and not the appetite to be feasted. Grisette, therefore, acts well her part. Flowers and fancy for the upper ten thousand, in the glow and excitement of evening and gas-light—but neither airs nor graces attend her, nor do flowers deck her hair as, by day-light, in the cool of the morning, she repairs to her accustomed stand, with her tin coffee-urn upon her head.

During the day, perhaps, she assists her mother, in —— street, who is a very respectable washer-woman, and highly esteemed for those exceedingly desirable qualifications, namely—the rendering of linen white and well starched. And thus, Mademoiselle Grisette fills up a very clever space of usefulness. Instead of degenerating into a more dawd, as so many beauties become during the unenchanting hours of day-light, lounging the time away, from sofa to rocking-chair, and from rocking-chair back to sofa again, with some trifle of a novel in their idle hands, Grisette, who does not know a letter in the book and, is thence fortunately secure against the seductions of popular *literature*, betakes herself, with hearty good will, to the wash-tubs: and *they do say* that her cousin Marie and herself have rare fun whilst splashing among the suds, in detailing the numerous conquests they (poor things!) supposed to have made in the flower market the evening before.

The Old French Market on a Sunday.
From *Harper's Weekly*, 1866.

Celebration of St. Patrick's Day

SATURDAY, MARCH 18, 1848

Here and there, in our city, even at the earliest hour yesterday morning, might be seen the usual green sprig in the cap or hat of the sons of Erin, signifying the advent of St. Patrick's Day. At about noon, the Hibernian Society, with their beautiful banners, (preceded by the "Star Spangled,") marched in procession through the principal streets. We don't think we ever notice a civic society that made a better appearance; the uniform of the members was a plain citizen's suit of black broadcloth; and their wide green badges contrasted well with this. The harp, Ireland's national emblem, was covered with roses; and the music played merrily as they moved along. It was generally acknowledged that they made a handsome appearance. As far as we have heard, everything went off finely.

There is something beautiful in the tenacity with which the Irish preserve their love of country even so far from it. If Old Ireland were flourishing and happy, we doubt whether this would be the case; and thus it is so commend-able, that, amid her griefs and oppressed condition, thousands and thousands of true heart still turn fondly to her.

———— ✦ ————

Hebrew Benevolent Association Ball
TUESDAY, MARCH 21, 1848

This ball, which was given last evening at the St. Louis, and for which preparations have long been making, exceeded in brilliancy our most sanguine expectations. As is well known, it was given for the benefit of the "Hebrew Benevolent Association," one of the most praise-worthy and useful institutions in the city. During the past year, when death and disease stalked through the city levelling alike the young and old, this Association was indefat-igable and very successful in its efforts to alleviate the sufferings of the unfor-tunate victims. It was therefore with joyous feelings that we viewed the great numbers last night assembled in the St. Louis.

As to the Ball itself, it was "superb beyond compare." As we entered the room, the brilliancy of the thousand-reflected lights—the tasty and rich dec-orations of the Hall—the unsurpassed beauty of the fair—combined with the excellency of the music—rather reminded us of some fairy assemblage in the Arabian Nights, than a meeting of poor "mortals of clay." In every respect—as much in the taste displayed in the arrangements, as in the number and beauty of the assembly—did this Ball equal any that has this season been given in this city. The refreshments provided were amply sufficient, and of a most tempt-ing nature. The arrangements, too, were so perfect, that not a single event oc-curred to mar the festivity of the joyous scene. Of the bewitching beauty of the ladies assembled we need scarcely speak.

The loveliness of the fair "Daughters of Israel" is too proverbial to need the praise of our pen; suffice it, that they fully sustained their well-merited repu-tation. But they were not alone in their glory, for the Christian maids assem-bled to the call of charity—rivalled them in grace and loveliness. Many were the large expressive eyes that every where shone upon us. Lovely were the rosy, peach-like complexions and clear rich olive *brunette* that every where encompassed us. Nor were the sons of chivalry less nobly-looking than the more delicate sex were fair. Where Venus is to be found be sure the Adonis is not far, nor if low silvery tones and soft beaming eyes are evidences, was Cupid himself absent from the scene.

The dresses were neat and becoming, and in many instances rich and magnificent. The air was ladened with Arabian perfumes, and the glare of jewels and dark flashing eyes were almost dazzling. Where every thing was so perfect, and where beauty so generally prevailed, it can hardly be expected of us to particularize. Indeed, were we to attempt it, the calls of perfection that every where existed, would draw us beyond bounds. Our joy of the whole was too ecstatic, and our admiration of the fair, *en masse,* too great to admit of a distinction, without, perhaps, being invidious; but if, at the exclusion of many that caused aching hearts, we mention one or two that rise in our minds like Naiades from the sea, we trust the fair excluded, though not forgotten ones, will remember that distinctions were made last night, and impressions left on other hearts than ours, that Time himself will never efface. We will, therefore, simply refer to those that, to us, appeared the most conspicuously lovely. Such were the Misses E——s, Miss V., R——s, Miss H——e, Miss J——h, Mrs. J——, M——s, Mrs. L., R——s, and in fact, so many crowd to our minds, that our columns would be filled were we to attempt to do justice to all. Suffice it, every thing was perfect, and all found a merry pleasant meeting.

———— ✦ ————

Health and Cleanliness
THURSDAY, MARCH 23, 1848

Q uery: If the authorities were to have all the streets well cleansed, regardless of expense—and individual owners and tenants would aid the good work by care, cleanliness, and a profuse use of the white-wash brush, even on the curbs of the walks—would it not have a powerful influence on the summer health of New Orleans?

✦ ✦ ✦

——— + ———

Sketches of the Sidewalks and Levee;
With Glimpses into the New Orleans Bar (rooms)

Daggerdraw Bowieknife, Esq.

THURSDAY, MARCH 23, 1848

It is almost with fear and trembling, "I take my pen in hand," to attempt the portraiture of this fearful son of Mars, whose very name is almost enough to

> —"Freeze my young blood.
> Make each particular hair stand on end,
> Like quills upon the fretful porcupine."

We do not say that our hero lives in New Orleans now, but he "used to did," and that's enough for a chap whose business is to make "Sketches." He lived here once upon a time, and flourished extensively—went to the Legislature and to Congress, for aught we know—that is, the Congress of Texas, while that "lone star" was shining with bedimmed lustre in the political firmament.

Squire Bowieknife emigrated, some years ago, to a village in Mississippi from one of the Carolinas. He was a limb of the law, and by dint of an abundance of swagger, in short time fought his way into notice. There are parts of Mississippi where a man may graduate into public favor, through the merits of gunpowder, with a rapidity that is astonishing. It requires a peculiar conformation and internal organization—a fitness of things, as it were—to constitute an individual who can thrive upon sharp steel and patent revolvers, but Bowieknife was the man, and "he went it with a rush."

Thence, he found his way to Orleans, and now has gone to Texas, followed by the ghosts of no less than six hale, hearty men, at least, that were such before his "bloody-minded" shooting irons made daylight shine through them. Never did man stand more upon a point of honor than he did: he would cavil upon the hundredth part of a hair if he thought a bit of a fight was to be go out

Tough Man with Bowie Knife.
From *Arms of All Nations* collectible card series, Allen & Ginter Cigarettes, 1887.

of his antagonist: and upon the most trifling misunderstanding in the world, he would attack you in a "street fight," or "call you out" and shoot you down, as though your life was not more value than a cur dog's. Oh, he was a brave fellow, and people were afraid of him, and we cannot wonder at it.

But it so happened, that the Hon. Daggerdraw Bowieknife was not, by any manner of means, so punctual in meeting his own little liabilities as he was in being first upon the ground to take his part in the murderous duel—in other words, he was one of those "d——d high-minded, honorable, clever fellows," who would rather shoot a man than pay him what he owed him. There are such men in the world, and our friend was one of them: they pretend to be the very soul of honor, but an honest debt, such as an honest man would pay with entire punctuality, these sons of *honor* "pass by as the idle wind, which they regarded not." One day, Daggerdraw sallied out from his office to take a walk into town. He was armed and equipped, though not "according to law," but he was, in common parlance, quite "loaded down to the guards" with fashionable killing tools. In each pantaloons pocket he carried a small loaded pistol: in his bosom, and within reach, was the handle of a large bowie-knife, weighing just one pound and a half, one of those murderous weapons more efficient than the Roman short sword, and equally serviceable at cutting or thrusting. Daggerdraw had done bloody deeds with it in both ways, as more than one individual in Mississippi had experienced to his sorrow. The said big butcher-knife had run the rounds of several street fights, and was the dearly beloved of its dreaded owner. Whether the personal prowess he displayed in its use was in violations of the laws of decency and humanity, and befitted him more for the society of desperadoes and professional cut-throats, is altogether another question. No man doubted the bull-dog courage of this disciple of Blackstone, but whether any of the sympathies of human nature, such as make man the being he is, had an abiding place in his ferocious heart, is not for us to say, though it may well be supposed there was none.

Yes, there he goes! and there is blood upon his shirt now, or at least there is revenge brooding in his thoughts, and ere long the life of some doomed one must pay the forfeit. He is not a bad-looking man either, being genteel enough in his dress and address but

> "There was a lurking devil in his sneer,
> That raised emotions both of hate and fear."

His eye was wild and restless, and there was a something in his brow that was repulsive. "And the Lord set a mark upon Cain"—can it be true that this modern Cain had his mark set upon him too? And yet there it was, the stamp and the impress of the cruel heart, legibly fixed on the very lineaments of the man's face, and no one loved to gaze upon him, for his features had that about them to freeze the heart of the beholder.

Why it is that a false sense of honor requires men, to face in deadly combat such as Daggerdraw, it were hard to divine. Perhaps they suppose, as Bob Acres says, that honor follows them to the grave. We are of opinion with Bob's servant, that this is the very place one might make shift to do without it, and that the honor and applause, such as it is, whips over to the adversary. Very well: Squire, take your grand rounds, and as you walk the streets, feel secure that men are afraid of you, but take good care and don't get afraid of yourself. I've heard strange stories about you—how that you never sleep o'nights: that you pace the long gallery of your boarding-house with restless and uneasy steps, and while others luxuriate in the blessings of "tired nature's sweet restorer," sleep is a stranger to your eyelids. I have heard that the lone and solemn hour of midnight is a terror to you, and that the ghosts of murdered Banquos will rise mentally to your vision, as a meet reward for your deeds of awful transgression, and your disregard of the injunction, "Thou shalt not kill."

Some men become noted, some are celebrated, and other, again, have the stamp of notoriety affixed to their names: such is the unenviable condition of him whom we have here sketched. He has made his mark through life, and it has been in the spirit of the pestilence and the destroyer.

———— ✦ ————

New Orleans Sabbath Recreations

MONDAY, MARCH 27, 1848

The sight of a New Orleans Sabbath—such an one as yesterday—is enough to prove to any stranger of Puritanical notions that the day may be kept in as orderly a manner here as in the cities where custom requires the squaring of one's conduct and looks by a sanctimonious code. People yesterday—hundreds of well-dressed women and men—turned out to enjoy the natural beauty of the day, and the respite which it always brings from weekly toil and cares. The churches had their attendants in the morning—and the squares and the shady sides of the streets in the afternoon. But it was from sundown till nine o'clock that the greatest pleasantness seemed to prevail. Then might be met with, in every thoroughfare, groups of ladies and men, walking slowly, and chatting and laughing merrily. Shall it be said that this was not a rational way of spending the evening?

———— ✦ ————

Sketches of the Sidewalks and Levee; *With Glimpses into the New Orleans Bar (rooms)*

John J. Jinglebrain

TUESDAY, MARCH 28, 1848

The subject of the present "Sketch" could never by any possible mischance be considered as "one of the b'hoys." "The lines are fallen to him in pleasant places," and if there is any peculiar blessings attached to "the ton," Jinglebrain has a chance to enjoy it.

You see him in St. Charles street, and in the haunts adjacent thereto, and you cannot fail to notice him as remarkably *distingué* in his air and appearance. His coat and his pants, his vest and his cravat, his hat and his boots are all remarkably "the thing"; and as you observe him at 11 or 12 o'clock in the morning, as he issues from some one of the fashionable *coiffeurs,* you would not be far from right in supposing that he had just made his escape from under the lid of a band box. His hair is "done to a turn," and every individual member of his side locks is in its right place, and is indeed, as slick as grease. His whiskers and his moustache are combed and anointed with some sweet scented unguent, and he snuffs the atmosphere of St. Charles street as though the very breath of heaven was unworthy of the patronage of so much clean linen and fine broad cloth, as well as a very extensive swell of personal pretensions.

Count d'Orsay, Patron Saint of Dandies, drawn by Daniel Maclise around 1830. Wikimedia.

Some poet or other—Shakspeare I think—makes allusion to one having small *pretentions* to manhood, that "the tailor made him"—and if ever an individual might disclaim maternity from the common unclean mother earth, Jinglebrain is that man, for clean clothes and bear's grease have made him what he is. Nor is it in our nature, or within the bounds of our present purpose, to cavil with any man because he dresses in a seeming and becoming manner; God forbid—for we ourselves luxuriate in clean linen and goodly raiment, and are made glad thereby: but that mortal man should feel puffed up in self-importance because of his outfit from the tailor-shop, and affect a pitiful superiority over his fellows, solely on the grounds of the fit of his pants and the sleekness of his hair, is marvellously beneath what we ought to expect from the dignity of human nature.

However, it is to Jinglebrain, not so much as a dandy, nor even as a conceited numskull that we now desire to paint him as he is, but as one of your do-nothing, nothing-to-do gentry who affect to hold all useful occupations in disgust.

Man is an eating animal, aye, a drinking one too—were it not so, the barkeeps and the restaurants might suffer. Man, we say, is an eating animal, and as such he needs occupation to furnish him the wherewith to buy bread and butter, and those little daily necessaries, such as food and clothes to wear. The merchant toils early and toils late, and not unfrequently carries his cares from the counting room to his pillow—the professional man is full of anxiety, and very often leads a life which is the opposite extreme from pleasure and repose. If we survey the streets of our city, we see the sons of toil in their various degrees and standing, and all active in business and bustle, and wherefore? Man is an eating animal and a clothes-wearing animal, and women and children need sustenance and shelter too. There is something noble in filling up an honest and praiseworthy sphere of usefulness—in furnishing our quota towards the requirements of good citizenship—but what sphere of usefulness does Jinglebrain fill up, what niche of honest industry does he occupy?

It is said that he had a wife once—people say that he had more than one, but that he has none *now* is just the truth and "nothing else." There are some little peccadilloes which it might be unpleasant to bring to light, and which would under such development exceedingly disturb the peace and dignity of our friend Jinglebrain—all these deeds and misdoings are wrapped in the veil of oblivion, or perhaps of an "alias," and now he sports his moustache and clean linen *per se,* and is a gentleman of leisure. He has an overflowing purse too, and every body knows how he shuffles and makes shift to keep it replenished. No man has greater horror of the restraints which a business occupation imposes, than this same dandy whom we are attempting to "Sketch." He has no ostensible occupation, no business office, no fortune that he has inherited, no "old man" of a father or an uncle who is very rich and very indulgent, and yet he always has a plenty of money—always flourishes in the most fashionable style and eats at the most expensive table.

Philosophers tell us of many wonders in nature—wonders of the earth, the air, and the mighty deep; but of all the wonders of a wonderful world, the way in which some people live is the greatest wonder yet. Jinglebrain boards at one of the crack hotels, and after a 10 o'clock breakfast, he patronizes the barber for an hour or two, and then *dawdles* about, as Fanny Kemble would say, until dinner. He plays a game of billiards, whiles away an hour at the green-room of one of the theatres, drinks at the most fashionable restaurants, and lunches at 12 or 1 o'clock in the most recherché manner imaginable. You see him promenading the streets, or driving dull care away with a choice regalia and a fresh newspaper, as he lolls in an arm chair on the portico of his hotel—he's a "gentleman" in a wonderfully good humor with himself and evidently feels his keeping.

Jinglebrain affects the critic too in literature—he pities the poor drudge that writes, but he condescends to notice productions. He twirls his moustache or puffs his segar with exceeding genteel nonchalance as he passes his comments upon some work of genius—and all the while too, he, Jinglebrain, is a numskull; in learning he has hardly passed "the rudiments," and if his pretensions could only be inspected, it would be discovered by a *minus* in the estimation of others. We have heard it said that our friend has but one standard of quality, and that is from the skin outwards. His gentlemen are made up of three parts: first, broadcloth; second, clean linen; and thirdly, of hair. No man without a moustache has ever been known to be recognized or receive a street salutation at his hands. Multitudes of those who knew him at other times and in other places receive no look of observation or recognition from his whatever.

What will become of Jinglebrain when he dies we cannot say. I am sure no one can tell. There are denunciations and there are blessings pronounced on the souls of those who do evil, and those also who do well: but what dispensation of mercy there is for those who have no souls, and who regard only the corporeal outside of the living man, we are by no means of sufficient wisdom to determine.

———— ✦ ————

The Nights of New Orleans
TUESDAY, MARCH 28, 1848

The nights of New Orleans are more than beautiful, that is to say, when the tempest does not cloud our sky. The summer nights of New Orleans! How lovely they are! In the pure blue ocean above, the moon "glides like a silver shield, which has been thrown by some pale warrior upon the sea of hope!" The glitter of the stars seems richer then, and their gleams flash with a sunnier lustre than those of the pale orbs of the North. The air seems burthened with health and hope, and as the cool, refreshing breeze sweeps along and fans with its almost noiseless wings the brows of those who woo its fragrance, one can almost detect the smell of orange blossoms and separate it from the aroma of the rose. Our calm summer nights! They are delightful beyond comparison, and in all that is connected with poetry will outvie in beauty the "lovely skies of Italy." Let no one go away without enjoying, even be it for an hour, the influences derived from the observation of our calm, sweet Southern night. Gentle Peace with starry wings then seems to spread her pinons o'er the world, and the healthful breeze sweeps by redolent with scents that are rich and pure.

———— ✦ ————

In the Wrong Box
TUESDAY, MARCH 28, 1848

Night before last, a gentleman whose face was decorated with imperial, whiskers and a moustache, took it into his hands to pay a visit to one of the balls down town. Our hero shut up his razors, washed the foam from his soap, and for a moment thought only of the bills that his customers owed him for the *barber-ous* vocation in which he was engaged. Two or three brandy toddies proved that he was at the head of all professions, and inflated with the idea, he boldly went on his way and entered the ball room. The gas lights streamed like the beams stolen from the trail of some brilliant comet, and music soft as ever sped from an Orphean flute, made the air redolent with harmonious sounds. The barber was entranced, and mentally resolved that he would never again shave for less than a dime! One of the nymphs who "waved her nimble feet upon the gay-deck floor," accidentally attracted his gaze, and soon became an object of his especial admiration. After a waltz, coffee was called for, and then cogniac and cigars. The unfortunate wight, after having drained, time and time again, the "flowing glass," found himself in the middle of Chartres street. How he had come there, he didn't know—that he had been in the ball room was a positive fact, but by what mysterious conveyance he had been place in his present position, he could not account for. He looked around him, and saw the houses dancing a gallopade—the signs were flitting up and down the street, and the whole vicinity seemed to be going round like a coffee-mill just before breakfast time. In order to preserve himself from falling, he grasped an iron lamp post; but to his imagination, the post was as slender as a weed, and he dropped into the gutter. Here, with eyes full of mud, he in vain looked for the polar star, which would give him the direction to his home; and after having by a miracle extracted a piece of potato-paring out of his left nostril, he sneezed as though he had taken "a huge pinch of Scotch snuff," and not used the "gentle titivation."

"Vere am I?" said he, as he dabbled his legs in the gutter. "Vere am I?" I know vere I was, but vere am I now?"

"Oh! I knows you, my friend," said a watchman, stepping up, "you're the person that slipped away from the Charity Hospital night before last. Now come along with me, and I'll take ye to the maniac department."

"Vere is de moon? I cannot see him—he must be down or up. Vich is he, my friend? Can you not tell?"

"Oh! I know your'e the man, and I've always heerd that crazy people was somehow afflicted with mooney feelins, and when she riz their sperrits would always go up. So, come along with me."

Charley firmly believing that he had hold of a crazy man, took him to the Hospital, and there the unfortunate barber remained all night before last. Yesterday he came to the police office, and said, "he declare he was not crazy, but zat he had loss his umbrell, and beg zat it might be refund to him."

The barber got his umbrella, and walked up the street with the gait of a crab with the rheumatism, swearing at every step, "zat ze next time I am take up, I wish I may be d——d!"

——— ✦ ———

Serious but Ludicrous Accident

TUESDAY, MARCH 28, 1848

There is but one step says a celebrated author "from the sublime to the ridiculous" and the truth of the saying, by applying the term "serious" in the place of the word "sublime," was yesterday proven. At about half-past 3 o'clock, P.M., a Dutchman, who no doubt had any quantity of schnapps on board, seeing the Pontchartrain Railroad cars coming towards the corner of Craps and Champs Elysées streets, endeavored to head them in the same manner that John Minor Botts endeavored to head John Tyler—that is, by going against them. The Dutchman whipped his bare boned steed until he came within a foot or two of the nozzle of the furious steam-engine. The poor beast, who seemed to have more respect for his own feelings than he had for those of his master, reared and plunged backwards out of the way of the cars. The suddenness of the shock threw the driver out, with the strong leathern reins twisted about his shoulder. After having been dragged several feet, the reins suddenly broke and the driver was pitched plump upon his head in the middle of a black oozy matter composed of mud and filthy water. Some gentleman ran to his assistance, and thinking from the blackened appearance of his face that he was a dead negro, raised him and placed him upon the banquet, whilst the blood was running from his mouth and nostrils. After pouring a bucket of water upon his face, the white man, became apparent. As he opened his eyes, his first words were not "Where, o where are my poor wife and children?—but, *"were ish mine horse and cart!"* He was relieved from further attendance immediately, and soon took the march for his home, where his gentle "frau" no doubt anxiously expected him.

---- ✦ ----

New Orleans in Mud
WEDNESDAY, MARCH 29, 1848

Yesterday morning the streets of New Orleans were completely enveloped in mud. It was n't common mud either—it was kind of swishey-swashey soil, that gave way ankle-deep at every step, and bespattered the pantaloons of all who trod upon it. It was indeed a "day that tried the *soles*" of those particularly who had on varnished leather boots. And then the rain came during the forenoon in torrents, and umbrellas jostled against each other with the greatest fury. Umbrellas, by-the-bye, seem to have a natural antipathy towards each other—they remain safe when it does not rain, but when it does, about half of their number are nowhere to be found, whilst the other half cause misery that is scarcely imaginable. Many a dual has had its primary cause in an umbrella. . . . The Levee, that muddy desert, was a beautiful scene for a man to look upon out of a window, but to traverse it was almost impossible. The wheels of the drays were almost buried in the soft composition, and the poor horses managed only to drag themselves along, and even then dray-pins and the whip were in requisition. Ship captains, the proprietors of sailor boarding houses, inspectors of customs and ship brokers, stepped over the muddy limits as carefully as though they were endeavoring to cross a precipice on a bridge made of blotting paper, or composed of newly laid eggs. As for the ladies, Heaven bless them! they did n't dare to venture out at all—no—not they. All the Cashmere shawls in Chartres street would not have tempted them to get their white stockings soiled by the "squash" of a loose brick. Altogether, yesterday was a day that was by no means pleasant to pedestrians, and we hope that the clerks of the weather, will not, if possible, combine rain with such mud. One or the other, as he chooses, but not both at the same time.

———— ✦ ————

Razors, Reason, and Resolution
FRIDAY, MARCH 31, 1848

I s there any poetry in turnips? The ghost of Walter Scott says "no!" Milton bids his daughters to hand him his spectacles, so that he may see out of his blind eyes, in order to discover what is going on. Copernicus chides his young son for having dared to supplant his father in astronomy, and Alexander the Great cried for a toy of a kingdom's destinies to play with. Oh, that elder Aleck! How sharply he cut among the nations of the earth!—his sword was like a scythe, and "he mowed them down like so many weeds," but he wasn't half so sharp as the *new* "Razor Strop Man" that we saw yesterday. He was a person that Nature had evidently intended for a "mock auctioneer," but had afterwards found out that she was mistaken, and doomed him to sell razor strops.

The new "Razor Strop Man" is none of your vulgar pedestrians. He wears a glossy suit of black, and indulges in a black silk hat with a piece of very black crape upon it. Moreover, he has a pair of spectacles on his nose, and his eyes look like those of a philosopher who is endeavoring to discover the difference between the tooth of a mouse and the optical organ of a flea. He looks wise beyond comparison, and if his wisdom only once sunk in, it would be the death of him beyond doubt. We saw the individual in question, yesterday, on St. Charles street; his basket, full of razor strops, was on the pavement, and a numerous crowd of spectators were congregated about him. He knew his profession, and every thing was as "slick as grease."

"Gentlemen," said he, holding up a razor strop in his hand, "I do not wish to speak, but I will relate a little circumstance that come to my personal knowledge. On the banks of the Hudson I met with a beautiful girl—the daughter of one of the proprietors of those princely palaces on the banks of that romantic river. Oh! it is a delightful land! In summer the air is like that of Eden, and the scenery rich beyond description. In winter, when the white snow covers the hills like a pure garment, the hall in which the lady of whom I have spoken dwelt, looked like one of the palaces on the banks of the Rhine. To make the story short, she was in love. A young man, handsome in person, and possessing all the attributes necessary to the happiness of woman, had chosen her as the idol of his heart. They met when the moon streamed down their silvery beams

The Original Razor-Strop Man.
From *The Life and Adventures of Henry Smith,* 1848.

and when the breeze was scented with the fragrance of southern flowers. They worshipped each other, and if they had been parted, death would have put an end to the beautiful scene. Well, gentlemen, they were married, and ere the honeymoon was over, the blooming bride became dissatisfied. What was the cause? Her liege lord wore his beard too long. And when they were upon the point of separating, I, luckily, happened to pass by. I sold him one of *these* strops, and the next morning he was as happy as a prince!"

The crowd dispersed, but each person said, or seemed to say, that *this* Razor Strop Man, was "some, and no mistake."

---- ✦ ----

Visit of a Distinguished Personage
WEDNESDAY, APRIL 12, 1848

Toward the latter part of yesterday afternoon, the *real* Razor Strop man— *the* man, we say—entered the Crescent office and deposited upon the counter one of his strops; as a last parting gift, we suppose, for he said he was going away from New Orleans.

Mr. Henry Smith, the gentleman referred to, (why is he not a gentleman, as well as other folks, who are richer?) is a singular instance of the force of perseverance, applied to what most business people would call small things. From a deplorable condition of poverty and disgrace, to which he was sunk some years ago by intemperance, he suddenly started forth, with but a few shillings of capital, as a vendor of razor strops. With a clean face, and a neat but not at all fashionable suit of clothes, he took his stand off against that busy corner of Nassau and Spruce streets, New York—then the Sun office. Determined to do his best, and probably expecting to make only a mere living, (on the profits of selling strops for a quarter of a dollar a-piece,) he stuck to his post manfully; and his ready wit, good humor, and the unfailing repartee with which he always turned the laugh on any of those ironical critics that a crowd produces, gained him customers fast and thick. In time, the same prudence and energy which lifted him out of his evil habits, led to his becoming a partner in a large and profitable factory for his wares, at Troy, N.Y. Let no one despise small profits!

MONSTER BALLOON—GRAND ASCENSION....Madame
RENARD has the honor of informing the public that she
will make her first ascension in the "Louisiana Balloon" on
SUNDAY EVENING at 4 o'clock precisely, from the corner
of Poydras and St. Charles streets, when she hopes to be
more successful than in her former attempts. She has made
great preparations to prevent accidents.
Office open at 2 o'clock P. M. . . . Price of admission, 50 cents;
children and servants half price.

Ad in the *Times-Picayune,* 1848 (recreated image).

"Servant" is a euphemism for "slave."

———— ✦ ————

Non-Ascension of the Balloon

MONDAY, APRIL 3, 1848

Yesterday evening, hundreds were congregated about the corner of St. Charles and Poydras streets, in order to witness the ascension of Madame Renards in her splendid balloon. The seats, we are compelled to say, were poorly filled; but the heart of the lady aëronaut seemed filled with enthusiasm almost to suffocation. Madame Renards had on a black velvet cap trimmed with ostrich feathers, and her silken curls dangled down her ivory neck. She also wore a blue bodice *à la militaire,* and a scarlet kirtle, together with a pair of white pantaloons trimmed with edge lace. She marched round her balloon with the air of a conqueress—but, alas! she was doomed to be defeated. The balloon was swelling with the weightless power that was to bear its tender burthen near to the confines of the realms above—the daring lady grasped the hands of several of her friends, as the mighty bulb expanded and expanded. The car in which she was to have reposed while ascending the giddy heights of air was brought to be attached to the balloon, and just as they were tying the ropes, the balloon "busted." The lady in question consequently did not go up; but, certes, her temper did not go down. Several small boys attempted to get a sight of the evaporated, ruined balloon, but the way that the Madame pelted them with brickbats would have taught a lesson to the gentleman in the primer, who, "finding that turf was of no avail, had recourse to stones." One of the persons who was engaged in some mysterious operation in connection with the "airy elevator" got his whiskers singed considerably by the flames that issued from the stove. The expectations of the audience went down when they found that the balloon did not go up.

———— ✦ ————

Who Shall Wear Motley?

MONDAY, APRIL 3, 1848

S aturday last was All Fools' Day. Now if it had been "kept," we doubt whether thousands of very worthy and honored folks might not, with propriety, have joined in the celebration. Why not? Are the fools of earth confined to the number whom general consent acknowledges as such? By no means. Indeed, the tallest specimens of the genus are to be found in a "respectable position" in society.

What is he who so fervidly worships the Dollar God—closing his heart to all beautiful enjoyments, the simple and the pure—that he possess more money, for the vile love of money alone? He may be a shrewd hand at a bargain; and perhaps his eyes are sharp enough to see the nicest shades of profit and loss; but he never enjoys his profit—he only accumulates. Week after week he toils on; wrinkles are sunken in his brows; the head and shoulders bend; the early thoughts and the old generous impulses become ossified, as it were; and soon his very face images the metal which he so adores. Ah, give him the motley!

Then that class—they pride themselves, some of them, on being very superior and select—who never sympathize with the suffering of weak and perhaps erring hearts; who disdain to stoop and comfort the son or daughter of poverty, because the suffering may have been caused by the victim's own imprudence; who never experience that most exquisite of pleasures, the consciousness of having alleviated misery, and done good to the distressed; are they *wise,* or shall we class them with—the others?

The mean man, and the wicked, are the greatest of all fools. For some fancied end, they forfeit both their own esteem and that of all others whose opinion is worth any thing. Give *them* the cap that towers highest.

Young ladies, who reject the hand of the man without money to marry money without a man, excuse us if we suggest that you too deserve a patch of the same varied cloth.

And ye frail vessels among men, who yield yourselves fully up to the dominion of poisonous and withering appetites; why did ye not celebrate last Saturday. It was your special time.

The furious in temper, scattering in one moment what years cannot recall; the squanderer, whose money leaves no sign of good done to him; the scowler, who looks ever on the dark side of humanity; the effeminate man, who develops not the uses of his manhood, (wouldn't this include old bachelors?)— the mere voluptuary, that gets to think women all frailness, and thus debars himself from domestic happiness, the purest bliss on earth; the glutton—the idler—the sneak—the bully—the fop—the man who don't take a newspaper, (or, taking it, don't promptly pay for it)—the politician, that thinks all people wrong who don't stand on his narrow platform—Ah! give a plentiful supply of motley to them all, for they could truly wear it!

------- ✦ -------

Day after the Election!
WEDNESDAY, APRIL 5, 1848

How often do we think of that simple word—"yesterday." The married man thinks of his marriage on *his* yesterday, the broker has his yesterday marked with "a white stone," and the successful politician his yesterday identified with many pages of foolscap. But *the* yesterday of the public was a day and no mistake. The features of the victors in the contest were radiant with joy, whilst the faces of their chop-fallen opponents, looked anything but beautiful. At about eleven o'clock, the successful candidates, dressed in their best, emerged from their dwellings flushed with the feelings attendant on victory." Ha! ha! my dear Jones," exclaimed one, "I told you *I* would be elected! Never say fail, my boy, act up to old Richelieu's maxim, 'never say fail.'" Oh, how cordially his friend Jones grasped his hand, and squeezing it in his vice-like fingers, remarked in tones full of pathos, "never was so glad in my life! I bet on *you,* and I won! Laud, if you had seen the fellers that was going agin you! I told

'em that *you* was to be elected, and no mistake, and they voted for you, and
nobody else!"

"Thank you, thank you! much obliged, but have got much business to attend to. See you again. Good bye—good bye!"

"But see here, Mr. Jinkins, that little situation that you promised me, what
about that?"

"Jones, business—particularly such as I have to transact, is important, and
must be attended to. I believe I did say something to you about a-a-a-a—and
when I get time I shall reconsider my opinion. Good bye, Jones! I'm in a great
hurry and must be off."

The 'sucked in' though of *his* yesterday, and the 'sucker' of his success.
"Cuss me," said the 'sucked in,' if ever I vote for him again, I wish I may be
d——d! Offered to give it to me, and 'taint much, no how; and now election's
over, he's jist as proud as a bed-bug that's been feedin' off the hide of a Con-
gressman! Didn't I spend his money liberally? Didn't I cuss his opponents, and
swear that he was the only man who deserved to be elected? Didn't I work like
a nigger or a tiger, for week for him, and when he hadn't no money to do the
'treating,' didn't I use to go borrow it for him? And when the election day came
on, who was the man that stood by him? Who was the man who give the 'sock-
dologer' into the face of Jim Brown? Who was it that crossed the names out of
some of the tickets, and put 'tother ones in, jist for his benefit? But it 'aint no
matter, and drinks nothin' but cold water, says, 'there's a good time a coming.'
I'll take an' pocket my difficulties, and say nothin' more about 'em!"

So saying, the gentleman who was to have been elected to a party office, with
a face that looked any thing but amiable, put his hands in his empty pockets,
and with pursed lips endeavored to whistle to the tune of "Begone, dull care!"

———— + ————

Strangers, Beware!
SATURDAY, APRIL 8, 1848

Our city is seriously speaking, the most moral in the Union. When we say
this we mean to infer that according to the actual population, there is

less crime committed here during the "business season" than in any other city
of the Union. Now, for instance, during the summer months, by referring to
the police books, it will be found that crime depreciates during that period at
least eighty per cent. The jails are almost empty—the work-houses have no
signs of life within, and the Recorders and other magistrates have abundant
time to enjoy themselves. But when autumn pokes in his jolly face, with cheeks
as reddened as his fallen leaves, and hair as yellow as his sun-burnt sheaves,
then let strangers beware. Pickpockets then, are as numerous as fleas in fly-
time, and as Jack Falstaff says—"in good troth, they then bestir themselves!"
In the winter we have the usual amount of murders, robberies, etc., which are
incidental to a populous city, but, in the spring time, the blossoms on the tree
of vice commence to open. Gentlemen, (who have very light fingers,) who have
been educated in their profession in the artistical schools of England, France,
Germany *and* New York and Boston, will certainly endeavor "to make a raise,"
each and every one of them, before they go to their summer quarters. Therefore, let strangers look out, and keep an eye on their pocketbooks, iron safes,
and all that "sort o' thing."

The Balloon Blow Up
MONDAY, APRIL 10, 1848

Yesterday it was advertised that a lady would ascend in a splendid balloon,
from a square on Poydras, near St. Charles street. At an early hour, hundreds and hundreds were in attendance. On the opposite side of the street, the
lookers-on clustered together like bees in hiving-time. "Here she goes!" "There
she goes!" were the cries. Presently a small parachute went up, like an umbrella
with a yellow cover. The delight of the audience, particularly those who did not
pay, was intense, and each one came to the conclusion that the Madame with
the mysterious French name, would, on this occasion, go up for certain, but
they were mistaken. Just about the time that the car was being fastened to the
balloon the Madame expressed a desire not to approach any nearer heaven—
so we are told. On this occasion the Madame had on a dress beautifully suited

to the steam that arises from a pot of boiling turnips, and like a fairy giantess, she took up a piece of scantling, and with her own fair hands belabored the person of a young gentleman who sat upon the fence, much to the delight of all who looked upon the performance. Just about the time that the "airy vehicle" was going up, it came down, but luckily, the Madame was not in it, but had she been in the car, her neck would have most "indubitably" been broken. Then "came the tug of war"—the b'hoys thought they had been fooled too often—and they tore down the boards of the enclosure, and seizing the unfortunate balloon, trailed it through the streets, and tore it into pieces not more than an inch in width. For a time, Poydras street, from St. Charles to New Levee streets, looked like a flower garden, so numerous were the red, green, blue and yellow fragments of the destroyed balloon. The balloon was totally destroyed by the gang who seized upon it, and its fragments scattered to the "four winds of heaven," amidst the shouts and jeers of hundreds who were in attendance. It is scarcely possible that Madame Renard will again essay to "go up."

———— ✦ ————

Bouquets
FRIDAY, APRIL 21, 1848

A mong the pleasantest features of New Orleans, that strike a stranger's eye, is the multitude of bouquets—beautiful ones—that are for sale at all the corners of the streets, and the entrances of places of amusement. These elegant bouquets, costing here only a dime, would in more northern cities bring the venders at least a dollar a piece.

———— ✦ ————

Lafayette Square
FRIDAY, APRIL 21, 1848

T his beautiful square affords one of the most delightful promenades in the city. At night, when the moon wafts down her silver lustre—when

Lafayette Square. From *Ballou's Pictorial,* 1859.

the green leaves of the streets within the enclosure, sigh as 'twere towards one another, then come forth the modern Romeos and Juliets of this, our gallant "Crescent City." Would that Mercutio were alive to recount the very tender things said by beings whose hearts were inflamed with love in that "same old square." Early in the morning, the lawyer of great expectations, but remarkably small practice, may be seen dangling with his client, and endeavoring to make him believe that without his assistance he must indubitably be ruined. At mid-day, the loafers, those lazy turtles, who float, with eyes half closed, upon the sea of society, may be seen lolling on the benches, ever watchful, however, that the police office is near. But "anan, anan!" as the waiter says to old Jack Falstaff, why don't the fathers of the city get some one to paint those hideous looking palings that surround the budding trees, and then, again, how much would it cost to have a marble, or even a granite fountain built in the middle of the square? The square is surrounded by buildings which possess much architectural beauty, and is in fact the most fashionable place of residence in the city.—The addition of a fountain would much enhance the value of property in the neighborhood, and afford much pleasure to our citizens.

✦   ✦   ✦

———— + ————

Vagrants

FRIDAY, APRIL 21, 1848

Where do they come from? Where do they go—those children of vice, wretchedness and woe? "Can the beauty of the rose be withered and scathed by the hot wings of the arid wind as it passeth by?" Yet, in the police-offices yesterday, there were many who, in a true sense of the words, "had known better days!" In one corner of the dock there was an old man, who ever and anon wiped his spectacles with his handkerchief, as though he wished to wipe from his memory the visions that glanced upon the mirror of his mind. He was a drunkard—the lowest of the low—but yet he sometimes blessed God; and when he put his spectacles into his pocket there was a moisture in his eye. Away went the old man, and, may be, took with him the history of his love and life to con it over within the chilly walls of the calaboose. . . .

In another corner there was a pale, thin-visaged woman, who sat shivering, as it were, and hiding her head from the audience by covering it with her apron. Her face bore the impress of beauty, and her soft, white, taper fingers told that once she had been a lady—and better than that, a woman! How changed the scene! This creature, once, perhaps, the idol of a lovely household, had become dishonored—dismayed and lonely. Even as one step is above or below the other, so sink we down or rise in the estimation of the public. Life has its steps—its days are but the rounds upon the ladder, like that seen by Jacob—which must carry the true and just to happiness and heaven.

———— + ————

The Old Cathedral

SATURDAY, APRIL 22, 1848

This venerable building was, on Thursday last, resorted to by hundreds of those who wished to show their penitence and humility. The old monastic church stood, as it were, aloof from the wings on either side. The temples

St. Louis Cathedral. This image depicts the church before its major rebuilding in 1850.
From *Norman's New Orleans and Environs,* 1848.

dedicated to the law—the higher Courts on the one side, and the Municipal
Court on the other—have been renovated, and now look like modern struc-
tures by the side of some monument of old. The tall, gray Cathedral, reared
its ancient spire to Heaven; but the towers wherein the bells that have tolled
the death-knell, and rung the merry marriage music of thousands, were silent.
It was a day dedicated to the "King of Kings"—it was the "Holy Thursday" of
Passion Week. It commemorated the occasion of the "Last Supper" of our Sav-
iour, who, when surrounded by his disciples, gave them his last earthly bless-
ing. There were over two thousand communicants kneeling at the altars, at
various periods during the day, and all seemed fully sensible of the solemnity
of the occasion. Grand Mass was celebrated—after which, many persons came
in to adore or communicate in spirit with the "Son of Man." In the niche upon
the right-hand side, stood a *basse relievo* of the Virgin and her Child. Upon a
table near by, was a bronze figure of the Crucifixion, and underneath a higher
portion of the altar, a cross, covered with purple silk, the color emblematical
of the blood that gushed from the wound inflicted by the spearman, upon the
person of the Divine Nazarene. On the other side, was a niche dedicated to
St. Francis; this was half covered with a parti-colored drapery, which entirely

concealed the face of the Saint, but underneath, there was an altar composed of the most gorgeous flowers—whose radiant beauties were lighted up by innumerable candles in silver candlesticks. The church was crowded by those devoted to the Catholic religion, and presented a scene that was solemn and interesting in the highest degree. Our dark-eyed Creole beauties, with their gilt-edged prayer-books in their hands, would walk in with an air that seemed to say that beauty was a part of religion. Dipping their taper fingers into the holy water and crossing their foreheads, they would then walk up the aisle and kneel down to prayer. We saw many women there whose garments betokened that some dear friend had not long been laid in the grave. They knelt before the picture of Christ carrying his cross, and prayed, no doubt, that they might have strength to carry theirs. Persons of all classes bent down before the shrine of Religion. There was the broken-hearted man of the world—the gray-haired man, whose feet were on the brink of the grave—the blooming girl, whose charms were budding into womanhood—and the wrinkled, care-worn widow, to whom love was but a memory. Then again, were the old servants of ancient families; and then ragged, pale-faced creatures, who looked as though they did not dare to approach too near the altar. The whole scene was beautiful and solemn, and calculated to impress the heart with the purity of virtue, and endow the soul with full reliance in the power of Him who rules above. Yesterday was Good-Friday—the anniversary of the Crucifixion. The ceremonies on this occasion were of the most imposing nature, and showed reverence and respect for the tortures endured by the God-like Hero of Calvary, for the benefit of a sinful world.

———— + ————

The "News Boys." A Street Conversation
TUESDAY, APRIL 11, 1848

Yesterday, at about 2 o'clock in the afternoon, whilst passing the corner of Common and St. Charles streets, we heard a confab, which ran as follows:

Jim Brown.—(A small boy, with a jacket, much too small for him, and a bun-

Two News Boys, by David Gilmour Blythe, ca. 1846–52.
Carnegie Museum of Art.

dle of papers under his arm.) "I don't care—I got as much right to live as you
has, an' I'll try an person that comes by!"

Tom Jones.—"Who are ye talking to? 'Spose I'm going to be fooled by a little
feller like you? Didn't I see yer ketch him by the coat-tail and drag him down
to the Werandah? 'Taint right, no how, and if you don't say so, ye'll git licked—
that's all!"

Brown.—"Look here, I'm little, but *you* ca n't lick *me!* I don't want nothin' to
do with you, 'cause I know who you are. Didn't I see you to-day sell a man who
come down the river, an old paper, when you ought to have give him a new
one? No, sir-ree! you can't come it—I'm little, but *you* can't lick me! I *pays* for
my papers!"

Jones.—"I aint got no time to talk, 'cause I got a good many to sell, but if I
ever ketch you comin' about my diggings agin,' you'll git flogged! You're regularly takin my customers away from me—and when I'm busted I 'spose you'd
like to see me in the House of Reffurage?"

Brown.—"I wouldn't like to see you no where's else, 'cause you think I'm not big, and I ain't, but I can lick you—you ——"

At this period of the affair Master Jones pitched into Master Brown. Their papers fell from beneath their arms, and to use a sporting phrase, they "closed." Jones, who was the bigger of the juvenile champions, "stood off," and occasionally gave Brown a pelt, but Brown returned it with more than ordinary vigor. After pummeling each other for a few moments, and losing each several copies of the different daily papers, the young gladiators were separated, much to the chagrin of those who took an interest in the fight. An elderly gentleman, tall and masculine in person, came up and pulled the Lilliputian combatants asunder. The little boy picked up his papers with one hand and whipped his eyes with the other, declaring all the while that "he was *little,* but he couldn't be *licked!*" The big boy stood upon his dignity, and offered his opponent "a rough and tumble," which he accepted. As they were going to work again, the gentleman, already mentioned, again parted them.

"Boys," said he, "why do you wish to quarrel? now—don't fight—it's very wrong, and cannot produce any good. My young friend, (addressing Brown,) what papers have you for sale?"

Brown whipped his eyes, and said in a tremulous voice, "Here is the Commercial Times, the Bulletin, the Picayune, the Delta and the *Crescent!*"

"I'll take one of each," said the old man. The little boy looked into the old man's face, and when he had received his money went to the corner, wondering why an old man wanted so many papers.

"Now my boy," said the elderly stranger, addressing the tallest of the two combatants, "what papers have you for sale?"

"Got all of 'em, sir," replied he in a dogged tone.

"Then give me the same number of papers that I bought from your young companion, and for the sake of an *old* man never quarrel again."

The money was paid—the papers were delivered; and the old gentleman, conscious that he had performed a good deed, went with a gladdened heart to his hotel. Ten minutes afterwards, Jim Brown met Tom Jones. "Tom," said Jim, "we won't fight no more—I didn't mean nothin,' but I was mad, and couldn't help it."

Tom replied, "Jim, look here, old feller, you and I is friends now—that old codger is a travellin' preacher, or somethin' of that sort—but we wont fight no more!"

The two boys shook hands, and shortly after the sound of—"'ere's the Bulletin, the Daily Crescent, the Picayune, the Commercial Times, the Daily Delta, the Mercury and the National!"—were shouted forth by lungs as fresh and buoyant as ever inspired the breath of youth.

———— ✦ ————

Sketches of the Sidewalks and Levee; With Glimpses into the New Orleans Bar (rooms)

Timothy Goujon, V.O.N.O. (Vender of Oysters in New Orleans)

TUESDAY, APRIL 4, 1848

There is in all cities bordering nigh unto the sea, a certain species of fish ycleped oysters, very much sold by certain individuals, of rare peculiarities, called oystermen.

In this goodly city of New Orleans, (albeit, not so very good either,) there abounds a class of worthy citizens named as above, and who exercise the office and administration of fishes of this nature, styled as we have said, oysters. The daily duty of these individuals—free citizens of a remarkably free city—is to vend by retail the interior fleshy and somewhat savory substance of these shell-fish, as above alluded to. The outer crust, or envelope of these, being of a tough, unyielding and indigestible quality, is rejected and thrown aside as worthless, nothing being eating by the children of men but the puffy contents thereof. To sell such, is the business and daily care of those called, in common language, oystermen—the French style them *ecaillé*.

It cannot have escaped the notice of the most casual observer of men and things, that the streets and well thronged thoroughfares abound in certain brick tenements, professedly devoted—not the building, but the occupants— to the preparing and rendering fit for the mastication of all and sundry reputable citizens—at least those who possess the wherewith to pay for them—these said shell-fish, fished up by the pair of iron claws out of the briny deep. These tenements, bearing aloft the outward insignia of their rank and condition, are to be found in the crowded walks of the city—and he "who runs may read," and he who is hungry may pass and be served, not only to his heart's content, but also to his stomach's, which is the best end of the bargain. We ourselves have refreshed and regaled the "inner man," many times and oft by those luxuriating viands compounded by those disciples of the illustrious kitchener, paying our quota of current coin meanwhile, and going joyfully on our way. But of late we have ceased in our visitations to these temples—finding that a repletion of the stomach and a similar condition of the brain-pan were always in an inverse ratio the on to the other. When the stomach was full of luxury and good eating, the brain was empty—barrenness and desolation prevailing throughout "the dome of thought, the palace of the soul." In such an extremity, having ever been taught to respect mind rather than matter, we have preferred to become even as one of "Pharaoh's lean kine," in order to have use and exercise of the said article of brain. Everybody remembers the story of the old Dutchman so happy and so contented, who said that "he chust eats and thinks till he's full, and then he shmokes and shmokes, and thinks about notin at all."

An Oyster Vendor.
From *London, A Pilgrimage,* 1890.

'Tis not, therefore, to these Epicurean depôts we refer, or the proprietors thereof—not by any manner of means: they are well favored men, which, as Dogberry says, "is the gift of nature:" they wear black coats and carry canes. These, in the strictness of speech, and the bounds of propriety, come not under the classification above alluded to. We refer to certain graceless *sans culottes*—no, not *sans culottes* either, literally, for that would be "most senseless and fit"—but in the political sense of the term: men, who, in the scale of the social thermometer, do not reach boiling point by any means. It was to this enterprising portion of the body politic that Timothy Goujon belonged. Long had he lived and labored in the cause of science, for he was a practical naturalist—perhaps you may say a *conchologist*—spending his days and his nights among the shell-fish—he was a vender of oysters.

Goujon made his advent in "this breathing world" in the city of Bordeaux or in some of the faubourgs thereof. His parents being grave and close-mouthed people—a national characteristic—very naturally placed Timothy, when he had come to years, at the occupation which he has followed through life—namely, a fisher and a vender of oysters. Of the particulars of his crossing the Atlantic, and finding himself erect, like other "featherless bipeds," here upon the levee of New Orleans, we are sorry we have no well detailed account. Neither he nor his parents before him were able to exercise in the art of chirography, and therefore, of the deeds of his early life—how many times with furious grasp upon the iron tongs he has dragged these unoffending fishes from their natal bed, or murderously thrust the knife into their bosoms, and torn them from their comfortable little homes—of these things we are not informed, and must therefore, with provoking brevity, remain as mute as the same commodity in which he so perseveringly deals.

We have heard that a year or two ago he involved himself in the rent of a small box of a corner shop, where his beautiful triangular lantern, covered with red worsted, and bearing the inviting inscription of "*Always Oysters, fryd, rost & in the shel,*" hung out by night as a point of local attraction to the hungry and wayfaring, both of which variety of worthies it is presumed every sizeable city contains. This speculation did not succeed and Timothy sold out his stock in trade, including the beautiful red worsted emblem of gastronomy, and betook himself independently to the Levee, like a gentleman, where he might breathe a purer air, and give exercise to his lungs, at the same time vending *viva voce* the inanimate quadrupeds which lay piled up with so much *sang froid* in his boat beside him.

Often, of a Saturday morning, we have heard the melodious, guttural voice of Timothy Goujon, in that place in the city of New Orleans where men and women do, at this especial hour of the week, "most congregate," namely, in the Market-place. There have we seen and heard the sentimental Goujon trill forth harmonious ditty in accents something like the following, though it would require a mixture of the French horn and the bassoon to grunt out the strain with any degree of exactness, especially the chorus: "Ah-h-h-h-h-h-h-h-h de var fine hûîtres—veni ici, veni ici—come everybody, valk dis vay—veni ici. Ah-h-h-h-h-h-h a bonne marché—so sheep as navair vas—toute frais—var fresh. Ah-h-h un vertable collection—veni ici tout de suite, toute l'heure, everybody—jentlemens and plack folks. Ah-h-h come and puy de veritable poisson de la mer—de bonne huîtres—Ah-h-h-h-h-h-h-h!"

Adieu, Goujon, sell your oysters, and pocket your small gains, and live quietly and comfortably, *chuqu' un a son goût,* and *chaqu' un a son gré.*

---- + ----

Sketches of the Sidewalks and Levee;
With Glimpses into the New Orleans Bar (rooms)
Mrs. Giddy Gay Butterfly
WEDNESDAY, APRIL 12, 1848

The interesting specimen of the "blessed womenkind," as Sir Walter Scott calls them, whose fanciful name stands at the head of the present "Sketch," has lived and flourished in "Orleans" for some length of time: but strange to say, the flight of years that acts so differently from what the poet says of distance—the one lending enchantment to the view, while the other takes all the enchantment out of it; strange to say that years, and the flight of years, had fallen harmlessly upon the feminine person of Mrs. Giddy Gay Butterfly. She was

—— we will not say how old. A man may brave the dangers of the ocean wave, may rush into the jaws of death while facing the cannon of the enemies of his country—may ascend in balloons, and may not presume ruthlessly to trifle with a woman's age—a pretty woman's age—when once she has passed the rubicon of thirty. The age therefore of this lady is a sealed book—"sealed with seven seals." One thing, and one only, we may venture to set down, or rather to detail in this our *sketchy-biography,* namely: that time had laid the very tips of his fingers gently upon her—he had to do this much in order to maintain his consistency for all things are subject to grow old and to decay in a world so transitory, so fleeting, so fluctuating as this.

Mrs. Butterfly had been a widow, but she was one no longer than it "pleased goodness" to keep her so. Old Major Butterfly is her second husband. We need not say that she is both giddy and gay—her name declares this to a mathematical demonstration—she never has been any thing else. Of course she has heart—a heart so overflowing with love that there is no space in it for passions or emotions of any other kind. She loves her children vastly—that is to say, she would jump into the river to save the life of one of them, or rush through flames of a burning house to their rescue, but whether her love for them is of a practical, serviceable nature, we shall see presently.

Older Woman in Sunday Attire. Wikimedia.

She loves her husband—yes, a little, and that's a good deal considering that she is yet in the bloom of early summer, while "chill November's surly blast" has already began to whiten the "pow" of the old Major. She loves her friends, at least those of them that love her, which is very natural; but she especially loves her own fair face and fairer form, and her exceedingly genteel feminine personality. Unfortunately, however, this passion of love in its reflex and other tendencies, has closed up the avenue of her affections for those simple, homely, domestic duties, domestic fondnesses, that go to make up woman as she is and as she ought to be. Unfortunately, we say, in the case of Mrs. Butterfly, love, in her, takes the form and shape of admiration, and we are only too sorry to make the unhandsome avowal that a love of admiration has swallowed up nearly three-thirds of her feminine nature.

There is a fashion in the world, of praising, rather say idolizing women, whether they deserve it or not. A sort of blind, Pagan idolatry of woman, because she is woman: that is, while youth and beauty blooms about her—for when "declined into the vale of years," the worship becomes more rational and very often the meed of well-deserved approval is then withheld. Miss Martineau somewhere alludes to this species of foolish idolatry, and reprehends it as equally unjust and injurious; and to tell the truth, the sensible portion of the sex have a hearty contempt for all fulsome adulation not founded upon real worth. Women are mortals, and as such, notwithstanding their "silks and satins fine," are wrapped up in imperfection, even as we are. Sometimes they are styled "frailty:" but this too is unjust and ill-natured, for "frail" as they are, they embody a good deal of all the excellence that human nature can lay claim to. But they are not perfect, no more than we, and to make "golden calves" of them were absurd. Let them stand upon their own essential merits, without any extra "appliances," and even then the foundation of their influence would stand sure and unshaken.

True, a fondness for admiration is one of the reigning traits of woman's nature—it comes natural to them as for men to use tobacco. It was the "besetting sin" of Mrs. Butterfly, as we have already taken occasion to advert to. Certainly, Mrs. B. was a pretty woman; divers of her friends have insinuated as much; the gazes of men have more than half assured her of the fact, and her looking-glass—'tis a flattering glass, that of hers—has completed the delusion. We say delusion, for anything that makes one rely upon mere looks to the exclusion of other matters—such as the cultivation of mind, and the fulfillment of a sphere of domestic duty—is a delusion, and one of the saddest kind. True, as we have said before, Mrs. Giddy Gay Butterfly was a pretty woman; but if she was, that was no reason why she should make a ninny of herself, by leaving undone things that ought to be done.

And pray, what does she leave undone? Don't she dress like an angel and flirt about like a seraph? These things she certainly does; but as we have before hinted, there were beneath the family roof certain "little ones," to brighten the soul's affections and kindle afresh the joys that cluster about "home." Brighten the affections, indeed! We must tell the truth if it kills us: Mrs. Butterfly was "a stranger in a strange land," so far as her own domestic hearth was concerned. She had a resting-place there—a sort of local habitation—but beneath her patronage and care, it was no "home," to call such. Other thoughts, other feelings possessed her breast, and there was no room for anything so homely as home. Ah! when we think of these poor, little, motherless Butterflies, we begin to realize some glimmerings of what the Scripture calls "sowing with the wind and reaping the whirlwind!"

There are some people in this world of inhabited creation that supposed—vainly suppose—that if children—little immortals in jackets and trowsers—only have a plenty of bread and meat wherewith to cram their stomachs, and a trifle of clothing withal, that the grand totality of parental duty, in all its length and breadth and importance, is abundantly fulfilled. As for the rest—why, the streets and the highways can open wide their arms and receive them.

Now, we might stop here and preach awhile, taking a text from Pope—

"Just as the twig is bent the tree's inclined."

But we must "sketch," not preach. 'Tis ours to loiter by the way-side, and cull, here and there, a flower, and not pretend to settle down in the big field and attempt to sow the seed and cultivate the soil. That from such a train of systematic parental neglect the little Butterflies should grow up into rankness and vileness, impure in speech and coarse and rude in manners, is not at all to be wondered at. Those who know how to trace causes to effects and effects back to their causes, could have confidently insured such a fate.

As for Mrs. Giddy Gay Butterfly, she is still true to her name and her nature. Her habitual disregard of the *res augustæ domi* has grown upon her; as years increase she, of course, appears less attractive, and will, no doubt, become soured in temper from such cause. It begins to be a great grief to her that her boys are so mentally and morally ill-favored. She wonders how it can happen that it is so, and visits with weighty indignation the school-teachers,

upon whom, of course, all the blame falls, that the children are not so "genteel" as Mrs. ——, her neighbor's—forgetful, all the while, that there has been
training in the one case, and the utter want of it in the other—forgetful that
the doctrine of the "silk purse and the elderly pig's ear" applies, in the case of
children, with exceeding peculiarity and force.

As there is but one Mrs. Butterfly in New Orleans, we have taken occasion
to give a "full length sketch" of her. Everybody knows that the generality of city
children receive excellent home education, and are all of them, every mother's
son, travelling safely in the "way that he should go."

———— + ————

Sketches of the Sidewalks and Levee; With Glimpses into the New Orleans Bar (rooms)

Patrick McDray

TUESDAY, APRIL 18, 1848

Stranger, perhaps you've seen a stout, hardy-looking Hibernian driving
cotton bales along the street. He's a jolly-looking fellow, somewhat pit-
ted by the smallpox, cracks his whip in a peculiar manner, and drives a good
horse—that's a Patrick McDray.

He's a clever fellow, this Pat; and by dint of hard labor and a plenty of it,
supplies his daily wants and the animal necessities of five of six small Pats, who
look for all the world like chips off the old block.

It needs no "ghost from the grave" to tell us whence came Patrick McDray;
the thing *spakes* for itself, by a brogue as unerring as the pointing of the nee-
dle to the pole. True, he has some idea of becoming a native, as he says, of this
country, seeing he likes it so well; but it is enough for our present purpose to ac-
quaint you, reader, that Patrick patronized the "Green Isle of the Ocean" when
he came floundering, like a great calf, into this round world of trouble, where—

> "There's nought but care on every hand,
> In every hour that passes, O."

A Proud Irishman.
From *Fun*, 1880.

In his own "swate" land he had endured the frowns of an ill-natured world for many years, and it was one of the blessed chances which occasionally visit the likes of Patrick McDray, that brought him safe and sound upon dry land on this side of the wather.

But not only in the matter of mate and dhrink, and clothes was Paddy made a fortunate possessor of "virtue, liberty and independence"—and all as a natural right and consequence of breathing the blessed air that blows through the vales and over the hills of our rightful land—but Pat, by his change of soil and climate, became a sturdy patriot at the drawing night of the election.

Well, we may trace Patrick McDray up on one side and down the other from his birth and birth place in the "swate Isle," which is to the millions, "swate" only in the "uses of adversity"; we may follow him, we say, from plain Pat all the way up to his present improved condition of *Mr.* Patrick McDray, who owns his own team and drives it like a gentleman. It is a remarkable thing how a man will pick up, little by little; only give him a plenty of work and sure pay, and industry united to "virtue, liberty and independence" will do the balance. But Paddy was otherwise united than to the three twin sisters we speak of—Paddy had a wife, and Bridget was her name.

It would be exceedingly unbecoming to invade the sanctity of the domestic circle; and we prefer to depict Paddy as he is, either in his daily character as drayman, or in his occasional duty at the polls; but our picture would scarce be complete without one peep at Bridget, for at home she was the very "sowl of the cause."

> "O Nature! all thy shows and forms
> To feeling, pensive heads have charms!
> Whether the summer kindly warms.
> Wi' life and light,
> Or winter snows in gusty storms,
> The long dark night!"

An unsophisticated child of nature was Bridget McDray, sure enough. She was a mixture of this same "kindly summer" and "gusty winter," being all brightness and sunshine and good humor when things went well; but on the other hand, over-darkened with storms, "gusty" enough when ills prevailed. A strange compound was Bridget's physiognomy—the extreme of good nature and honest frankness was there, and yet as vexations are abundant in this "world of care," and abundant too in proportion to our yielding to their sway, there was to be seen in her visage the trace of a moral storm where furious passion had raged and left its lines in her brow and in the drawing down of the corners of her mouth. Naturally frank to a fault, yet, notwithstanding, "they do say" when her "Irish gets up" Bridget is "rale Tipperary" over again and can flourish a broomstick or her tongue with equal rapidity and violence. O but she's a jewel of a wife, is Bridget when "she gets in one of her ways."

Patrick thrives well; he pays his day and way like an honest man, and take good care of his horse Cashel, and this shows him to be a gentleman. He puts on his Sunday clothes when Sunday comes, and takes a walk upon the Levee by way of a variety, and when his wife Bridget "gets high" he just drops quietly out of the way and waits till the breeze has blown over, and this shows him to be a man of wisdom, for in the one case a multitude of words would only have "darkened counsel," while giving Bridget the whole house to herself, peace was speedily declared, there being no enemy to encounter.

We take our leave of Patrick McDray, wishing him success in life and a heap of it.

———— ✦ ————

A Walk about Town: By a Pedestrian
WEDNESDAY, APRIL 26, 1848

G ot up early from my bed in my little room near Lafayette. The sun had scarcely risen, and every object seemed lazy and idle. On some German ship moored at the levee I saw about a dozen stalwart sailors with bare legs, scouring the decks. They seemed to be as happy as lords, although their wages are sometimes not more than six dollars a month. . . . Saw a negro throw a large stone at the head of his mule, because it would not pull an empty dray— wished I owned the negro—wouldn't treat him as he treated the mule, but make him a present of a cow-skin, and make him whip himself. . . . Saw a poor long-shoreman lying down on a bench; had on a red shirt and blue cottonade pantaloons; coarse brogans, but no stockings. He had spent all his money in a tippler's shop the night previous for grog, and when his last picayune was dis-covered to be gone, he was kicked out of the house. Thought that there were some landlords who deserved to be bastinadoed. . . . Saw a shipping master riding at full speed upon a small pony. He would have been willing to have freighted every ship in port, if he could have been "elected." Saw him go on board a vessel, and come off again, with, in all probability, a flea in his ear. He kicked the pony in his sides, and after dismounting went into the nearest grog-shop. How he kept "his spirits up by pouring spirits *down.*" He didn't get the freight of that ship. . . . The sun had just showed his golden face above the gray clouds of the horizon, and bathes with lustre the distant scenery. Now come the bustle and business of the day. Shop-keepers are opening their stores; ste-vedores are hurrying on board their respective ships. Those stevedores! they are for the most part honest men, and, physically speaking, work harder than any other class of the community. Many of them have little tin kettles on their arms which contain their simple dinner repast. When their work is over they get their "bones," and then separate for their different homes to woo "tired nature's sweet restorer"—sleep; or mayhap to spend their day's earnings in a grog-shop. . . . There's a big, red faced man walking hastily up the levee. He's a Customhouse officer, and is hurrying on board his vessel for fear that if not there by sunrise, the Captain may report him to the Collector. . . . Went into St. Mary's Market; saw a man, a good old man in a blue jacket and cottonade pantaloons, with a long stick of sugar cane in his hand. Wondered who he was, and much surprised to find out that he was a lawyer of some repute. At the lower end of the market there was a woman with a basket of live crabs at her feet. Although she loved money, she had no particular affection for a press from the claws of the ungainly creatures that she handled with a pair of iron tongs. Saw the "cat fish" man, who declared that his fish were just caught, and were as tender as a piece of lamb. Went up the Market and saw rounds of beef, haunches of venison and legs of mutton, that would have made a disciple of Graham forswear his hermit-like appetite. . . . Came down town—shops all open—and heard the news boys calling out the names of the different papers that they had for sale. These boys are "cute" as foxes and as industrious as ants. Some of them who now cry out "ere's yer ———, here's the ———, here's the ———," may in time be sent to Congress. . . . Went down town further—all was business and activity—the clerks were placing boxes upon the pavements—the persons employed in fancy stores were bedecking their windows with their gaudiest goods, and the savory smell of fried ham, broiled beef-steaks, with onions, etc., stole forth from the half unshut doors of every restaurant. . . . Passed down Conti street and looked at the steamboat wharf. It was almost lined with steamboats; some were puffing off steam and throwing up to the sky huge columns of blackened smoke—some were lying idle, aid others discharging sugar, molasses, cotton, and every thing else that is produced in the great Valley of the Mississippi. Came to the conclusion that New Orleans was a great place and no mistake. . . . Went still further down—visited the Markets and saw that every luxury given to sinful man by sea and land, from a shrimp to a small potato, were there to be purchased. Came home again and took breakfast—tea, a radish, piece of dry toast, and an egg—read one of the morning papers, and then went about my business.

+ + +

———— ✦ ————

To the Seekers of Pleasure
SATURDAY, MAY 6, 1848

M any persons who are in the habit of profoundly thinking on the un-
certainty of human life, will agree with us in the belief that to-day is
Saturday—a day named after that old cannibal, Saturn, who not only ate up
all of his own flesh and blood, but afterwards swallowed several small planets,
in order to provide rapid digestion. Now, we Orleanians, are a working people, and believe it nothing wrong to take a little innocent amusement, even on
the Sabbath. Now, if one wants to enjoy a thrilling breeze, to inhale the scent
of Spring's newest flowers, or taste a delicious ice cream, let them go to the
Carrollton gardens. If they want a level road, where the bloods and the b'hoys
"most do congregate," and where the pompano actually cry out in piteous
terms, "please let me be broiled," let them go to the lake end of the shell-road.
If they want to be whizzed down at the rate of forty miles an hour, to Lake
Pontchartrain, let them get in the cars, go to the Washington Hotel. Messrs.
Kennedy & Co. have every delicacy of earth and ocean on hand.

———— ✦ ————

Carrollton
MONDAY, MAY 8, 1848

W e noticed yesterday that the different trains of cars running from
here to Carrollton, were densely filled. One of the most delightful
resorts in the immediate vicinity of the city is the Carrollton Gardens. Those
who like fish should go to the Lake—but those who like fresh air and flowers
should go to Carrollton. We learn that expensive preparations are being made
by the lessee of the Hotel for summer visiters.

✦ ✦ ✦

———— ✦ ————

Steam Stronger Than Shot
FRIDAY, MAY 12, 1848

W hat a beautiful steamboat, and, oh! how lovely the cabin is," whispered one lady to another, last evening, as they entered into that portion of the "floating palace."

"Hello, old hoss!" exclaimed a Kentuckian, who had just given his rife in charge to the barkeeper—"How do you do? When did you git back?"

The stranger—a tall, famished-looking man—replied, "I got tired, and got back yesterday; and as quick as Heaven will let me, I 'm goin' home. Them Mexicans is worse than the potater rot: I fout with 'em and cussed 'em; but it aint no use' they 're licked and they aint licked—but, just so sure as my name's Tom, I'm done with 'em."

At this moment, two gentlemen, enwrapped in the highest style of military costume, entered the cabin. They bowed respectfully to those who were present, and then, after having selected their state-rooms, unclasped their swordbelts. "A pleasant voyage, General," said one; "The same to you, General," answered the other—and the heroes shook hands, and thought of gallant deeds, of greener laurels, and greater triumphs.

The engineer has pumped up steam to an extraordinary extent, and suddenly he lets it off. Oh, Heaven! the noise was like that of the snorting of ten thousand whales, mixed with the brays of about a hundred and seventy-five John Donkeys. The Generals who had breasted balls and bulletins looked aghast and quivered from top to toe. One of them, the most distinguished, sought refuge in the cabin, and broke the wash-bowl. The other took to his heels, and after having run about half a square, it is said, hid himself behind a cotton bale. The Generals could stand Mexicans, and misery of all kinds, but they could not stand the idea of being blown up. The gallant vessel, however, would not explode, and, in a short space of time, all was happiness on board.

✦ ✦ ✦

———— ✦ ————

A Sabbath Sketch: Or, Going to and Coming from Church

MONDAY, MAY 15, 1848

The weather during the forenoon of yesterday was beautiful. Early in the morning the air was as cool as though it had whirled and danced around an iceberg in the Arctic ocean, and then been mellowed slightly by a tropical sun. The few trees, and they are more valuable because they are few, swung their pliant boughs, richly laden with green leaves, to and fro, as if in joy. The sweet May wind swept through the streets with a merry sound, and the flowers seemed to partake of its healthful influence. All was redolent of life and gaiety—the sun shone down with unclouded splendor, and cast a golden shadow on the streets and "all that in them were." At an early hour the Sabbath bells rang for Sunday school, and in a few moments after, hundreds of children might be seen wending their way to their different houses of worship. Little girls in white slips, and Leghorn hats trimmed with flowers, walked the pavements as daintily as fairies. Young boys, clothed in neat costume, might be seen walking arm-in-arm, with prayer-books and catechisms in their hands, whilst many an anxious parent's face glimmered through the window, in order to see that the young rogues did not play truant. When they met in the schoolhouse, they were caressed by their teachers, and then the words of wisdom were expounded by those who made it a labor of love to guide into the paths of peace the young, untutored mind. The halo of heaven will rest upon the heads of those who are in heart true teachers in the Sabbath School!

The little ones—the mothers and fathers of a future generation—have all gone by, and the bells have ceased ringing. Now comes another class.—The young clerk, who all the week has been engaged in the tedious business of selling dry goods, comes out from his domicil as fresh as the first daisy of spring. His boots are glazed, and contrast admirably with the snowy whiteness of his pantaloons. He wears a black coat, and a gay vest, whilst suspended from his neck there is a bright gold chain, attached to a watch of the same material, which is concealed in a pocket made in that portion of the waistcoat that lies directly over his heart. Wonder if the heart beats in unison with the tickings of the watch? With the air of a lordling he walks up to the bar of some one of our fashionable hotels, and in an authoritative tone calls for a "julep," which he invariably drinks after he has taken off his kid gloves.

Yonder, coming down the street, is a knot of the sons of the "ould Emerald Isle." You can detect them by their quaintly cut blue coats and tarnished brass buttons. They are hale, healthy set of men and many of them are tolerably well to do in the world. They are going to hear their pastor preach, and will no doubt return home much edified with his discourse.

It is nearly eleven o'clock, and the Sabbath bells again commence ringing. How musically they sound, and with almost human intonation, seem to invite the wayfarer to the house of worship. Just as directly after twilight on a calm summer's eve, the stars, one by one, trip into the blue aisle of the sky, the fair ones of our city appear in the streets. See yonder lovely girl with the beautifully moulded form, cheeks slightly tinged with the rose, and languishing eyes. She shades her face with her little purple silk parasol, and looks towards the ground. She is going to church to see somebody. As she passes the corner, a young man exclaims "Mary!" She takes his arm, and they go in a different direction from the church. They want to get married, but mama is proud, and papa is rich, and poor Edward has no chance to see his sweet-heart, only on Sunday, when she goes to church.

There comes a wealthy old merchant, with his wife hinged to his arm. He goes to church because his wife makes him go. She says "it's so respectable," and he is obliged to submit. He may govern the market in some instances, but she governs him; and he is forced to leave his ledger to read the litany. When the minister talks of the sacrament, the old merchant thinks of sugar; and when the crucifixion is mentioned, his thoughts are dwelling on the price of cotton. "William," inquires the old lady, whilst they are going home, "what was the text?" "Don't know, Maria, but think it was the Missouri, with four hundred hogsheads of sugar consigned to me—no, no don't know what it was; but walk fast, for I want my dinner." "Ah, William, that's always the way you talk! What will become of your poor sinful soul when I'm dead and gone?" "Don't know—'spect it will—go down Old Levee street, and pay that note for $675 tomorrow, else it will be protested."

Church is out, and scores of young men are standing on the pavement, eager to catch a slight at the fair maidens as they come out. That sweet looking young lady, who leans upon the arm of her gouty sire, accidentally brushes by a young gentleman with moustachios. By some ledgerdemain a tiny billet-doux is slipped into her little white hand, and is hastily transferred to her bosom. Poor old father is none the wiser, and knows not of the wily pranks of the daughter he calls his "darling little puss."

The humble widow, clad in sombre black, who has lost all that was dear on earth, walks by the side of the stately matron arrayed in gorgeous silk and dazzling jewels. The poor decrepid man who leans upon his stick, trudges slowly on behind the stalwart form of healthful manhood, and thinks of the old time when he too had the vigor and muscle of youth. The old and the young—the rich and the poor, come side by side, from the house of worship, and who shall say that they have not been benefitted by observing the Sabbath?

———— ✦ ————

Public Squares
MONDAY, MAY 15, 1848

The Place d'Armes and Lafayette Square were, yesterday, the resort of hundreds of young children who came to enjoy the fresh air, and the healthful exercise of "jumping the rope." For the most part the little sprites were accompanied by their nurses, who like foster mothers, took care of them with all the tenderness of parents. The scene was highly interesting. Little boys launched their kites into the calm air, and fairly screamed with joy when they saw them ascend high above the tops of the tall green trees. The little girls, as beautiful and sprightly as the attendants who waited on Queen Mab, tripped their "light fantastic toe," and make the welkin ring with their merriment. Altogether it was a scene delightful in the extreme. The green sward, the beaming countenances of those around, the pleasant breeze that crept through the foliage of the trees, and the radiant faces of the children, were enough to have even made a misanthropist smile.

✦ ✦ ✦

A Nineteenth-Century Omnibus.
From *Scribner's Magazine*, 1871.

———— ✦ ————

A Night at the Terpsichore Ball: By "You Know Who"

THURSDAY, MAY 18, 1848

A strict adherence to the truth compels me to acknowledge that I am a bachelor, whether young or old, handsome or ugly, rich or poor, I will leave your readers to guess. I am, however, like all bachelors, one from inclination, not necessity. As all philosophers have acknowledged that every one can be suited to their minds as regards the selection of a wife, why I should be an exception to the general rule, arises no doubt from the fact of my being a resident of this city of epidemics, and she *somewhere* else, with no likelihood of her ever getting here, so I have settled down as comfortable as circumstances will admit, joined the "Old Bachelor Society," intending to prove my constancy towards *her* by marrying *nobody*. If this ain't satisfactory and self-sacrificing on my part, and sufficient to immortalize me, I will *keel* over and expire.

Japhet in search of his father never had more difficulties to surmount, obstacles to contend against, and incidents to befall him, than I have had in my efforts to find *her.* I did not cease my labors night nor day, as my portfolio will prove, but all in vain; my supplications were useless, my efforts fruitless, my dreams and fancies of no avail. The following incident befell me in one of my exploring expeditions after *her.*

'Twas Saturday evening, cool and pleasant, just the kind of night for a dance, as I found myself with a few friends, comfortably seated in the Lafayette car. "Who knows," so ran my mind, "but what I *may* see *her* this evening? Nature may repay all my labors by showing me the one she intended to share *my lot.*" And a thousand other fanciful thoughts flitted through my mind, when "Gentlemen will please make room for ladies," assailed my ears from two or three stentorian voices. My gallantry would not allow me to remain one second after this appeal; so I got up on deck as best I could, amidst the yelling of a crowd of the b'hoys trying to sing "Old Dan Tucker." I was about taking a seat, but finding some *three inches* of the thickest kind of dew on the bench, I *stood* it the balance of the distance.

At length we arrived at the end of our journey. The Trojan horse could scarcely contain more persons than that car; they were pouring out from all sides and in every direction. I followed the crowd. Arriving at the ball-room I imagined all trouble and inconvenience ceased, for that night. Poor deluded being! I forgot I had a hat, and that I should provide a place for it. I did so, but I suffered some. The postoffice on advertising days was nothing to it. When I was clear of the crowd, I requested one of my friends to squeeze me into *shape* again; I felt as flat as a pancake. Did you ever put on white kid gloves—the delicate *little* creatures—without wishing they were never known? If you did not, I did, that night. In the hurry of the moment I bought sevens instead of nines. I pulled; I pressed and pulled again. No go. I was determined to have them on or burst. After a while I did both. Although my hands did look like *cracked dumplings,* I didn't care; so I put my *hands* behind my back and made my first *debut* amidst the chivalry, beauty, loveliness, and exquisite grace congregated in that social hall.

The room was overflowing with the beauty of Lafayette, with a sprinkling from New Orleans and Carrollton. A promenade was in order when I entered, and I watched each graceful form and lovely face; as they approached like sylphs of some fairy tale, in plain, fancy and mask dresses. Each one, methought, was more lovely than the other; but no, the object of my heart,— she who has caused me so many sleepless nights and restless days,—she whom I have seen so often in my dreams and imaginings, was not among the un-masked. I rose from my seat with a heavy heart, walked into the ——— and took a drink of lemonade *without* any brandy in it. On my return, a cotillion was in motion. I looked upon it with stoic indifference—*she* was not there, and not being there, the place or persons had no charms for me.

While musing to myself that I would emigrate to Europe or China—get wrecked, perhaps—find her on some barren, isle, etc.—I caught a glimpse of what I considered the very pink of perfection, in form, grace and movement, in fancy dress. Doctor Collyer would give the world for such a figure. My eye was riveted to the spot. My head began to swim. I saw none but her. A mist surrounded all the others, while she moved about in bold relief. She turned. I saw her face, radiant with smiles, ecstasy, delight. "'Tis she!" I ejaculated, as if tossed by a pitchfork, and caught the arm of a manager, to introduce me. He didn't know her. It was her first appearance in the ball-room. I imagined it an auspicious coincidence. It was also my first appearance. Seeing a gentleman conversing with her, I watched my opportunity, and seeing him alone, I re-quested him to introduce me. Never saw him before in my life; but what cared I—my case was getting desperate. He willingly consented; and off we started towards her. To describe my feelings while approaching her, is impossible. I was blind to all but her.

The agony was over; she spoke; and the deed was done; I found that she was every thing I imagined—accomplished, pleasing in her manners, agreeable in her conversation, well versed in the authors, from Dryden down to James— including all the intermediate *landings*—passionately fond of music, she said; and by her musical voice I *knew* she could sing. I was happy in every sense of the word—delighted beyond measure. She kindly consented to promenade— would carry me through a cotillion if I'd go—but, knowing nothing about the poetry of motion, I had to decline; and she—noble, generous creature as she was!—preferred rather to talk and walk than dance. I admired her, nay, I will confess, for the first time in my life, I felt the "tender passion" creeping all over me. *I was in love!* I could not restrain myself. Candor compelled me to speak openly—I told her I had been looking for *her* since I was 18 years of age. "Looking for *me!*" she exclaimed with astonishment. "If not you," I answered, "some one very much like you." She guessed my object, saw and understood all, and invited me to call and see her.

I was, in my own opinion, as good as a married man—at length my toils and troubles were to cease—I was about to be repaid for my constancy, by having the one for my wife that nature intended. Just at this moment where, in any other place I would be on my knees, the gentleman who introduced me, came up to us and said "*Wife,* ain't it time to go home?" "Yes, *my dear,*" she responded. So taking his arm, casting a peculiar kind of a look at me, and bidding me good night, they left me like a motionless statue on the floor. The perspiration flowed down my cheeks like rain drops—the blood rushed to my head—my face was as red as a turkey *rooster's*—I was insensible. Some of my friends, seeing my situation, carried me into the —— and administered another lemonade with a little brandy in it, which revived me very shortly. I jumped into a cab—in one hour afterwards I was in the arms of Morpheus.

It is very evident she was *the* one; and yet it astonishes me how she could take her present husband for me. There is no similarity, whatever, between us. She was still young, and no chance of being an old maid; while he appeared as careless of his wife's charms, as I did of his existence.

I wish them both much happiness, altho' I am the sufferer by it.

--- ✦ ---

Sketches of the Sidewalks and Levee;
With Glimpses into the New Orleans Bar (rooms)
Doctor Sangrado Snipes
THURSDAY, JUNE 29, 1848

We are told that the Northern colleges—medical colleges—send forth into this "breathing world" some thousand odd doctors per annum.

And we might almost continue the quotation and say that they are not only sent forth into this scolding, money-making world, but are also

> "Scarce half made up:
> And that so lamely and unfashionably
> That"—

they do their work very badly sometimes, that's all.

A thousand doctors! Set it down at a thousand—may be it's more—though this is monstrous. A thousand doctors—young doctors, turned loose like Samson's *foxes* with fire brands to their tails, carrying devastation into the cornfields of the Philistines. Turned loose, we say; making broad their *diplomas* even as the Pharisees of old made broad their phylacterics, that they might be seen and employed of men—of men, that is to say men in the sense of mankind, including women as well; for it was not for the favorable smiles of the gentler sex, perhaps all men would turn philosophers, and send physic a begging.

Our friend Sangardo Snipes, M.D., was "duly armed and equipped according to law," with a sheepskin as big as a breakfast table, couched in Latin which himself could not understand, but which "being interpreted," meant that he was a DOCTOR "fitten" to go to work with pill, poke and powder, and so physic the folks *secundum artem;* enjoying the right, privilege and especial immunity of making out his bills to suit the state and condition of this patients' purses. Dr. Snipes "graduated." He reached the point of rejoicing, and was entitled, and, according to the statute, dubbed "Doctor"; and straightway, being seized with a fit of philanthropy, or something else, packed his goods and chattels— his medical books and medical physic, and his precious box of medical bones, (faugh!) and with the remnant of a very lean purse, made tracks to the southward and westward, and landed safely and soundly upon the Levee in New Orleans; in which noted city he tacked up a shingle intimating that he was "death on fits," and soliciting, according to the usual formula, a "share of public patronage." No one ever thinks a hard thought upon Dr. Snipes as a two legged, bread-eating, clothes-wearing animal like the rest of us, or doubts the propriety of his having "wherewith to eat and to drink, and wherewithal to

Old Saw Bones. Vinegar valentine card, 1860s. New York Public Library.

be clothed"; the "world owes him a living" he is pleased to say, and our Doctor is "bound to have it."

Long time ago there lived in a distant part of the world, called Germany, one Baron Wenzel, a noted oculist, who made it his business to examine into people's peepers and perform certain needful operations thereupon. To effect his object he had a numerous array of weapons in the shape of couching instruments, formed form iron and steel, which like "villainous saltpeter," was dug form the earth. Baron Wenzel was a famous man in his day—he could see further into folks's eyes than they could see themselves, and by means of his sharp pointed instruments he could make daylight not exactly shine through people, but could make or had made it disappear out of them. "I do recken," said he one day while lecturing to a whole bevy of young oculists in embryo, "that I must have spoiled a *whole hat full* of good eyes before I got into the way of operating to advantage. Experience is every thing, gentlemen: go forth and do as I have done, and then kindly and as honestly as I have to you, report to me the result of your labors." He was a miracle of frankness, that Baron Wenzel, and I fear we shall never "look upon his like again."

Reader, look forth into the open air: see thou yon green tree stretching its giant arms towards heaven, and clothed with rich verdure. Well, just such a personification of greenness is any one of these thousand new born M.D.'s, with our friend Dr. Sangrado Snipes among them. Like Baron Wenzel, he has to learn in the school of "practice" and experience, and as he can't always say of his physic as Lamepdo did—

"I've tried it on a dog, so there's no danger!"

He must need essay the Galenic art upon the doomed sons and daughters of men. The Doctor is even now in the full tide of "experiment," (whether successful or otherwise is another question,) and if anything ails you, you can call him in; he lives No. ———, and will be happy to physic you—only, I say, take care, and ere you swallow the bolus think of Baron Wenzel and his "hat full of good eyes."

Dr. Snipes is really a clever, good sort of fellow, and I'm anxious to give him a lift. He tells me that every pill he administers is gilded, and that his "newly invented patent draught" is like old Boniface's ale, "as smooth as oil and as strong as brandy." Whether, like the illustrious patron of Gil Blas, whose patronymic he bears, he uses "his lance," as my good old Aunt Kitty calls a lancet, with happy effect, I cannot say, but, judging analogically, I should presume so, for he dips deep into the pocket when he gets a good chance. To see him sitting at his office door, in the cool of morning, some one of these summer days, you would hardly suppose there was any of the *ars diabolocus* in his composition. He is rather tall in person—wears straps to his trousers, and glories in a pair of big whiskers. With his feet upon the door cheek, conning over the morning "Crescent," you may see him almost any time after breakfast. As he puffs away at his cigar, you may suppose that visions of ipecacuanha and broken bones float gingerly across his imagination, and fees, in the shape of pleasant $50's and $20's, seem already, in fancy, to fill the vacant spaces in his pocket-book.

> It were vain to seek for the
> —"lurking devil in his sneer.
> That raised emotions both of hope and fear,"

and no one would suppose there was "terror in his looks," any more than there was in the lean Cassius. And yet—but why should we

> —"a tale unfold, whose lightest word
> Would harrow up thy soul—freeze thy young—
> Make thy two eyes, like stars, start from their spheres—
> Thy knotted and combined locks to part—
> And each particular hair to stand on end,
> Like quills upon the fretful porcupine;—
> But this eternal blazon must not be
> To ears of flesh and blood."

Therefore, smoke on, my Doctor; read your paper "with what appetite you may," and let your fancy luxuriate in the prospect of big bills. I'll not tell on you. Your mistakes have been a mere *lapsus,* or can readily be cloaked under the charitable veil of science ("falsely so called,") and perhaps will never be called into account against you. I remember once noticing a very handsome fowling piece over the door of a medical friend's house. He was an aged man—now gone to his rest—and was sometimes inclined to be witty. "Why, Doctor," said I, "I was not aware you were inclined to field sports." "Neither am I," said he; "thank God, I'm innocent of all lives, save in the way of my profession."

We make our best bow to Dr. Sangrado Snipes, and hope he may live a thousand year; and if we ourselves can keep out of reach of his "grape and cannister," we think our own chance for his desirable maximum much greater than, under different circumstances it might be.

New Orleans, June 27.

———— ✦ ————

Sketches of the Sidewalks and Levee; With Glimpses into the New Orleans Bar (rooms)
Old Benjamin Broekindown
WEDNESDAY, JULY 12, 1848

There is hardly any thing that is really what it appears to be." So sayeth our friend and beloved arm-chair champion, Dow, Jr.—but so sayeth not the world. Hope lends its bright wings of fancy to many of the fond delusions of this otherwise "dull, inferior clod," called earth, and more people than Mr. B. Broekindown have, in the winding up of a lengthened career in life, been obliged to sit down flat on the ground and write with the end of a stick, "Vanity of vanities, all is vanity."

Our friend was, as may be surmised, a merchant; that is to say, he had been during and active and laborious life, an honorable member of that pursuit which too often "lends the word of promise to the ear but breaks it on the hope." He had been a merchant; aye, and if there is a vast and visible distance between him who deals in large quantities and the retailer who vends the same commodities by the picayune, with a "La Guapa" to boot, our fallen friend was entitled to all the immunities of a so-called "monied aristocracy." I saw him the other morning wending his way slowly and sadly down Magazine street. I had known him in other places and other days. I knew him when his situation was thought to be most enviable, and every body, the ladies in particular, was glad to be smiled upon and nodded at by so rich a man. Alas! for such a vanity-shop as this world is; very few would care now to run after yon poor decrepid old man, tottering upon his stick, and creeping along so lonely and forsaken. Observe him—there is a cast of sadness in his face which it is really painful to behold!

Broekindown's case has nothing peculiar in it, or uncommon—only that he was a broken-down man. People said that "he had seen better days," and some such sympathy (from the lips outwards) they did vouchsafe to bestow upon a ruined and bankrupt man. But the voice of real sympathy was rarely heard, and many, perhaps the most of those who knew him, or rather, who knew of him, said somewhat sneeringly and with an appearance of satisfaction, that pride was always doomed to a fall, and that perhaps he was hardly to be pitied, as he was rearing his children to inch high notions—that a govern-

An Old Pauper.
From *Punch*, 1841.

ment so democratic as our own should not endure such distinctions, and that one man was as good as another—that for their part they were not averse to some little pulling down in society, as there was ever so much eagerness to climb up and make a grand appearance over the humbler neighbors—that the ways of the world were entirely too arbitrary any how, and that wealth was getting to have an undue influence in a country where "all men are born free and equal." These, and views and observations of a similar tendancy, often amounting to rank *agrarianism*, were volunteered by sundry envious individuals who being themselves among the "outs," necessarily hated those who, in regard to fortune, might be regarded as the "ins."

Poor Mr. Broekindown! he now lived upon a trifle of an annuity which his wife (provident woman!) had secretly procured for two or three thousand dollars—money given to her when money was plenty, to purchase an outfit of new and more fashionable furniture, and which she wisely (foolishly, some said) bestowed as above named, continuing the old finery a year longer. O, she was a woman of a thousand, that! This little annuity, thus purchased, served now to "keep soul and body together," in a very humble and unpretending manner of life. Though poor and apparently friendless, this excellent woman was in time of extremity one of those precious friends which that sex so often "when pain and anguish wring the brow," prove to be. Rising superior to her condition and to the force of adverse circumstances, she became a pattern of christian resignation and christian hope: and often declared to her heart-stricken husband, that "though the grave had closed upon all her brightest earthly promises and though fortune had vanished away as the vapor, and her butterfly friends had all gone too, yet she verily believed that a kind Providence, while it chastened, was present to comfort her; and her faith, in a brighter and better world, and the joyful promise of getting her children again together there, was infinitely more consoling, more heart satisfying, than all the expensive gayeties and real emptiness of fashionable life." Poor woman! may-be she was right; and if she was not, and it was only a delusion that possessed her, we cannot but admire her philosophy and courage.

Some year ago, the thing was very different with the Broekindown family. O! could you have paused a moment in your walk, as you passed the door of that sumptuous dwelling in Walnut street, Philadelphia, on some evening of revelry, and observed the glare and show and brilliancy of much light—carriages driving up with loads of proudly-decorated Misses and Madames, and twirling off at a tremendous rate—the sound of the piano and the hum of merriment—you would have thought that there at least the favors of fortune were fixed and sure. It was a sight!—and many a one was fain to cast glances of envy and dissatisfaction at the grandeur of a few and the squalidness of the many. But fortune, if she is arbitrary, is also fickle. I had not seen my ancient friend for a long time—not, indeed, since one evening in December, 1834, when I attended a most brilliant fête at his princely mansion. As we met here in this distant city, and recognized each other, we grasped the hand of ancient fellowship in sadness and silence. Of course I had heard of the family reverses, and it would have been cruel as well as useless to have uttered one syllable of inquiry or explanation.

Broekindown is too old even to attempt to "repair his fortune," as the word goes. His great object, during the energetic portion of his life, was to amass wealth and to live in splendor: and there is very little prospect now that he can be even a tolerably happy man. His moral and intellectual nature has been permitted to lie in him unimproved, and, unlike his excellent wife, his faith in spiritual comforts and joys has scarcely a form of substance sufficient to hang a hope upon. If he were a younger man, the happy resiliency of human nature would enable him to overcome his troubles, and to shape his course in life anew. He might then see that the entire end and aim of man is not merely to lump together much wealth, or to live in a fictitious glare and glitter of much show, but consists mainly in the development of his moral and intellectual nature, and the cultivations of those principles which, when improved, are always a source of enjoyment in every grade and in every situation of life. Of all the neglected axioms which men "know by hear," there is none more true than that which declare our truest happiness to consist not in the desire after a good deal, but in contentment with a little; and that "he who wants much, will rarely be satisfied." In the business occupations of men, there is none whose temptations are greater than the merchant's—none who are led to forget that

> "Man wants but little here below,
> Nor wants that little long."

It is a fact difficult to be realized, in the case of our fallen friend, that he who reveled in his thousands, and to whom hundreds was "a very small thing," should even come to experience the "want of a dollar." But it was nevertheless true; and they who cast, not their "bread," but their wealth "upon the waters," are oftentimes obliged in sorrow to feel the force of the Scripture sentiment, "Let him that thinketh he standeth take heed lest he fall." The fluctuations of trade! Ah! true, the "fluctuations of trade!" And following upon the heels thereof, the vicissitudes of life, and the uprisings and downfallings of families, the sorrows, the fears, the dread, the waking up out of wealth and finding one-self penniless! Has anybody ever taken the trouble to watch the workings of a commercial community through a term of years? Something of the kind we have seen, and the blanks to the prizes were rather startling to weak nerves. But we grow serious, finding ourselves moralizing over much, but it is the fortune and the fate of our friend that thus made us contemplative; and besides, in these our "Sketches," we cannot promise to be always gay; life has too many stern realities to be facetious always; therefore, when we write, reader, for your edification, we will follow the plan laid down by the poet Burns:

> "Perhaps it may turn out a song—
> Perhaps turn out a sermon."

——— ✦ ———

Sketches of the Sidewalks and Levee; With Glimpses into the New Orleans Bar (rooms)

Samuel Sensitive, Part 1

SATURDAY, JULY 15, 1848

Samuel Sensitive was once one of the happiest fellows in "Orleans." Never, even among the crowd of young men who have such good opinion of themselves, was there any who had a better notion of his own cleverness than Sam. He held the highly important station of first clerk in the mercantile house of Messrs. Pork, Produce & Co., in one of the busiest streets of this very dusty city.

He had flourished in this establishment "going on" three years, and each season as it passed by, found Samuel constantly upon the improving scale. He came, I have heard, from one of the interior counties of Tennessee: his parents, who were clever, poor people, started this notable son off from home at the age of eighteen, to seek his "etarnal fortune" in distant parts. They had given him a "mighty slim chance" of an education, but fortunately for Sam, they had, as

Sir Anthony Absolute says of his son Jack, "begotten him before all his brothers and sisters," and being the first scion of the stock, was consequently a well-
favored and remarkably clean limbed young man.

Samuel had seen the world before he alighted upon the streets of this city:
he was an "entered apprentice" to Squire Muggens' store in the village of ———,
all in the State of Tennessee, as we have said, for a full twelve months before he
"cut stick" for parts unknown. Add to that, he had grown into intimacy with a
chap by the name of Jones, a tailor, from New York, I believe, who had come
like a god-send to the citizens of this village to set the fashions for them. Under the tuition of Jones, our friend Sam learned the true use of his legs and his
neck, namely, as appendages to the outward man for the genteel disposal of
pantaloons, and cravats. We may say, therefore, that Samuel, the son and earliest scion of his father David, knew something of the world before his descent
upon these regions below—these lower regions.

Another fortunate circumstance combined to establish the foundation of
his fortune—a disciple of the far-famed Dolbear came opportunely through
"them parts," teaching "rectangular hieroglyphical penmanship," for so said
the man's advertisement. Sam placed himself, bone and muscle, under the tu-
torship of this perambulating professor of the chirographic art. He was an
apt pupil, and it was soon found out that the village of ——— could no longer
contain an individual of such singular accomplishments; so, as we have before
intimated, Sam left and came South. Handsome in person, well grown for the
years, skilled in the mystery of dress, and, withal, a real dabster with a steel
pen, what could hinder him from making a figure in the world, provided he
had a stock of modest assurance sufficient to back him?

The city of New Orleans is a noble place for a young man of prepossessing
appearance—that is to say, there is a fair opportunity here offered for decorat-
ing his exterior. For a year or two, Sam's salary being small, he was content to
"live within his means." He had never yet learned to sing the song, sung and
practiced by so many—

> "How happy's the soldier, who lives on his pay,
> And spreads half a crown off of sixpence a day."

But ah! for the seductions that awaited Samuel Sensitive. I don't know but it is rather a misfortune than otherwise for a young man to be good-looking. A pair of squint-eyes, a stumpy nose and tallowy hair, might enable a young chap to make money "by the operation," or rather to save it, which, political economists tell us, is the same thing. But this wasn't Sam, for he was not to be sneezed at in the outward man, especially after his maiden whiskers and moustaches had reached their envied maturity. His previous tutorings under the tailor Jones had initiated Sam pretty well into the rudiments of dandyism, and now an increase of salary enabled him to know a little more of the

"Bliss beyond all the Minstrel has told,"

That lies in the cut of a vest, or the adaptation of a pair of "tights" to the next extremity of "man proud man." Nothing would now suit his immaculate toes but French boots at ten dollars a pair, and other items of outward gear in proportion. He spent more money in tooth-brushes, and fine-scented soap and segars, year in and year out, than would have kept his good old mother in sugar and coffee and tea; and a single year's account with his tailor was more than it had cost his good old Tennessee daddy for his whole family of fifteen children clean up to the time when they shoved out in the world and began to do for themselves.

I once knew a plain old North Carolina famer who was in the habit of saying that the difference between a "heavy crap of corn and a light crap wasn't so much as some folks fancied." His philosophy of the matter was in this wise: that when grain was abundant prodigality was very apt to ensue, where in the time of scarcity "they took mighty good care of the key of the crib." So it was with our friend Sam; he, who at first strove hard to make ends meet by eking out a little to go a great way, now by the use and abuse of fine cloth and shoe leather, contrived to make his eight hundred a year go no further. A man's expenses in a great city have a good deal of the gumelastic about them—you may stretch them out indefinitely almost, and you may contract them into the smallness of nothingness, so to speak, if you should change to be straightened in income.

"And if our lot be very small
'Tis prudence to enjoy it all."

Yes, so it is, but that is no argument why eight hundred dollars should be spread over the same surface that one-fourth of that amount formerly was, or that because of the abundance of temptation, the bounds of our yielding thereto should be determined only by the extent of our means. But so it was, and Sam spent his eight hundred per annum, and did it joyfully. There were tailors' bills, and shoe-makers' bills, and hatters' bills, and jewellers' bills; and then there were a thousand daily items in the way of theatre tickets, and billiards, and ten-pins, (Sam was a horse at ten-pins,) as well as feeding and drinking and smoking. But a change came over the spirits of Sam's dream, and "in the course of human events" Sam *fell in love*. Of this, however, we must defer our narrative, at least for the present, as well as the account we have to give of Miss Julia Katydid, who came like a visit of mercy to Sam, involving him, not as never man was involved before, but involving him as the sons of men very often have been involved, and will be, we suppose, until the end of all things—namely, first in the meshes of love, and then, as a very common, almost necessary result, into the web and entanglement of matrimony. But of this more anon.

———— ✦ ————

Sketches of the Sidewalks and Levee; With Glimpses into the New Orleans Bar (rooms)

Samuel Sensitive, Part II

TUESDAY, MAY 2, 1848

It is a fact sufficiently self-evident, neither to be gainsaid or in any manner to be disputed, that there is a deal of sweetness in the nature of a woman. Samuel Sensitive had fallen in love with one of the sex, and her name was Miss Julia Katydid.

It was a present to Julia, that Sam had, with due consideration of the consequence, resolved to abstract forty dollars and upward from his oyster and billiard account, and bestow it in a beautiful, enameled, filigree, inlaid morceau of *bijouterie,* whose value intrinsically, *per se,* was perhaps about six bits. Sam loved Katydid, and was very anxious, by all honorable means, to draw upon himself the heavenly influences of double-distilled blessedness in the shape of a sweet woman's love. For this purpose he set to work according to the manner and form in such cases "made and provided." "'Twere long to tell" the extent and the variety of Sam's amiability upon this occasion.

It was a lucky chance for the head clerk of Messrs. Pork, Produce & Co., that the star of Katydid rose upon his moral horizon, for he was posting the turnpike of iniquity in one of the biggest omnibuses that belong to that popular line. But mesmerism, in the shape of Cupid, made his "passes" at Sam, and speedily he was a "gone hoss." Julia Katydid was a young lady with bright eyes, very bright raven ringlets, very dark, and an alabaster neck, and a very nice chin with a dimple in it. Wasn't she pretty?

She was a niece of some good lady and she had a mother—who *was* a mother, and had brought up this feminine jewel of loveliness in a manner to develope the exceeding grace of nature pure and exalted as those best beings whom, in our dreams of fancy, we fondly suppose to hover about the abodes of innocence and peace. Those who only know women in the haunts and kennels of sensuality, are widely ignorant of the real nature of the sex, and while profligacy tends so purely to debase and "imbrute" the soul, as Milton says, the kindly influence of female innocence is like the quality of mercy itself, distilling like the gentle rain from heaven, and is indeed "twice blessed" whenever and wherever it is exercised.

It is a curious discovery that a young fellow makes when he becomes sensible of the existence of what is poetically termed "a heart." He is sick and he isn't sick; something is the matter, and he hardly knows what. He sits and sighs, whilst visions of blond lace and fancy ribbons, to say nothing of "love darting eyes and tresses like the morn," flit before his imagination, and render him very qualmish indeed. Sam never made so many blots in his day-book before, and once when he should have written "Dried Herrings," in copying an invoice, his pen insensibly traced the fair characters of the name of "Julia Katydid." He even tried to write poetry, saw beauty in the moon and stars, was frequently seen by the watchman to wander along the Levee, humming to himself "O meet me by the moonlight alone," or apostrophizing a bale of cotton in words like these:

> "Had we never loved so kindly;
> Had we never loved so blindly,
> Never met and never parted,
> I had ne'er been broken-hearted!"

Julia, it seems, had lately gone off up the river on a visit to some friends, and the self-same post to which the steamer was fastened when the fair Katy-did stepped foot on board, was like "stoned urn and monumental bust," to Sam. He couldn't have thought it possible that a big post should have gained so upon his affection, and as moonlight he stood there leaning up against the aforesaid romantic piece of timber, and gazed out upon the mighty Mississippi, which was running at that time pretty full of drift wood, Sam did feel sad, sorrowful and sober-hearted enough.

But why spin out a long story? for a long one could be told of the courtship of Sam and Katydid. Let is suffice to say, that through the benign influence of a very woman, a "change came over the spirit" of the young gentleman's dream,

A Sensitive Young Man.
From *He Knew He Was Right*, 1869.

and he who was once the prince of good fellows among a crowd of roysterers in an evenings' carouse, and could laugh the loudest and longest, and emptiest, was made a different chap of as soon as

"His dream of life from morn till night,
Was love—still love."

Why lengthen the recital? Katydid was not inexorable, neither had she a heart of adamant, harder than the nether millstone. She, being wooed, was in due course of things, won, and I can show the house where they live—that is, Sam and his wife Katydid. He visits the Levee no more by moonlight, not he; he stays at home like a decent worthy citizen, as he is. He loves Katydid, and has reason to bless the hours when she smiled and winked, and half-confessed that she loved him. The merchantable firm with whom Sam was brought up, opened wide their business arms, and took him in. Altogether, Sam is looking up in the world. Who will not say that it was not that same bright-eyed Katydid that made a man of him?

———— ✦ ————

Sketches of the Sidewalks and Levee; *With Glimpses into the New Orleans Bar (rooms)*

Miss Virginity Roseblossom

TUESDAY, JULY 25, 1848

We have a fancy, perhaps an odd one, of trying to body forth upon paper this solitary specimen of old maidism. Like some of those rare birds that fly out seldom, and even then are difficult to catch unless you put salt upon their tails—or like some streaming comet shooting athwart the sky, rarely visible and then to awe and to scatter dismay—like either one of these in its rarity is the character that heads our Sketch of this morning.

How long Miss Virginity had hung upon the virgin stem of celibacy it cometh us not to say—certainly all the days of her life, but how long a duration that was is the question. For ourselves, we would rather undertake to "summon spirits from the vasty deep," or to beard the Ghost of Banquo, or sing the song of "double, double, toil and trouble," with the witches of Macbeth around their infernal cauldron, than to go to work with coolness and self-possession to cipher out the years and months and days that have plodded onwards since the being of Miss Roseblossom first begun. There is only one hint that we dare make, and hardly a hint—she was a school girl at the time of the battle of Bladensburg, and the figure eight did not occur in the year of her birth.

This is a curious world we live in, and man is an inquisitive creature: he wants to know and he will know of the ebbing and flowing of the tides, the revolutions of the heavenly bodies, and of the rise and progress, social and political, of the kingdoms of the earth: but besides these there are other matters and things that would be worth knowing, if they could by any ordinary possibility be found out. Among these is the why and the wherefore of such instances of single blessedness as that of our present Sketch—why the virgin thorn still adheres to the tree of celibacy—why and how it happens that old maidism plants her unwelcome foot with an iron heel upon the fading remains of young maidism? Women do get married—this fact needs no argument to substantiate it, nor need we travel far for substantive evidence of the fact. They do so for diverse reasons—mainly however, that it turn out in the calendar or their personal history that the *right one* comes along, and where duty calls 'tis theirs to obey. They are willing to lose their individual identity, so far as name is concerned, and even in a legal sense, become as nobody, when they take upon them the appellation of those good household gentlemen who rejoice in the dignity of husband. All this is clear enough, and the rationale of the problems is not difficult, running somewhat in this wise: Two individuals of either sex meet—they experience a certain "drawing towards" as Monsieur would express it in bad English—they are sensible of the touches of what is popularly and tenderly called Love. After many meetings and partings, some sighing and hesitating. A B tells B C in flattering words that the only way to settle and arrange this tender difficulty which has arisen from too manifest a "drawing towards," is to join their hands and their fate, and to travel onwards together in the journey of life. B C, all so blushing and so tearful, says "oh, no," means "oh, yes," all the time. They marry and commence life, sure enough, with brave and hopeful hearts and honest hands. Providence has ordered this matter all right, for without this thing of Love, who would encounter the pains and penalties attendant upon reading a family? But these old maids—that's what we were talking about—how comes it that they have left to "pine in want," unmated and unmatched?

It is the hardest thing in the world for a man to talk on subjects like these without trampling on somebody's toes—but we have the enquiry to solve: why did not Miss Roseblossom marry, that's the question! She might have done so sometime between the occurrence of the battle of Bladensburg and the death of Bonaparte—one would suppose so, at all events, for she could not have been thus antiquated always—though really, in our short recollection, she has come up to the bible standard, of "neither variableness, nor shadow of turning." For years and years I've known her—the same prim, precise, pitched up peculiarities of physiognomy. She never married, and her name is Virginity Roseblossom still. Same said that it was an early love affair, that was in the way—"blasted hopes"—"faithful till death," etc. I've no confidence in any such tiddle-taddle, and rather think the story was promulgated by herself to salve over the real state of the case, which was a certain want of pre-requisites in the said lady:

Cupid Turning Away from Old Spinster.
Vinegar valentine, ca. 1900.
Western Kentucky University.

"the voice of the charmer, charming never so wisely," was not one of the feminine attributes of Miss Roseblossom. Indeed, the tones of her voice and the features of her face seem to have clubbed together to destroy her matrimonial fortune, and prevent her from getting a husband. It was the "sound of brass and tinkling jingle," as I once heard a backwoods brother misquote scripture—it was that hand-saw voice of her's, and that peculiarly vinegarish aspect of nose, mouth and chin, to say nothing of those "angelic" eyes, that upon occasion could look daggers and darning-needles at any unfortunate that should chance to fall under the category of her disfavor.

In the mesmerism of human sympathy there is the same kind of polarity as occurs in physical magnetism—we have the positive and negative poles; the one a polarity of attraction and the other a polarity of repulsion. Poor Miss Virginity Roseblossom! her's was all of the repulsive order, and the sound of her voice acted as a species of "flying artillery"—those who were not killed by the shot, were scattered in dismay. The majority of womenkind are not so— blessed be the stars that superintend the affairs of mortal man for it! As wives, mothers, sisters, daughters, O, what a sphere of blessedness is thus filled up! When lovely and loveable there is nothing upon this wide, breathing earth can approach the desirableness of woman; but as if to show us that even our best estate is bad, and our choicest comforts are imperfect, we see this same being, who else is the object of our adoration, we see her, when grown oldest in years and soured by neglect—we see her, formed as we all acknowledge, to sweeten the cares and soothe the sorrow of man, when grown fretful and unlovely, one of the saddest thorns that ever afflicted the mortal condition of man. In this respect, woman is like many other things in this curious world—the good are very good; the bad are hardly bearable. Good poetry and good painting are pleasing to the taste and give elevation to the soul, the bad and indifferent of both are equally dégoûtant.

Miss Roseblossom seems to have forgotten, or never to have learned, this one grand fact—that in the fancy the sexes have for one another, the first upris- ing of emotion is always from an indefinable something of witchery in her own sex. If that indefinable charm be not "thar," there arises no flame, no kindling, "no nothing" called, in the tender language of young ladies, Love. The woman that supposes she can be domineering in her voice, her manners, and her looks, and yet retain her persuasive power of conquest, makes one grand mis- take, and falls wide of the mark. We read in Scripture of the lion and the lamb lying down together, but it was the lion that put on the lamb-like ere the thing could be accomplished. In chemistry compounds will often form from very dissimilar ingredients, as for instance the union of oil and alkali to form soap; but generally speaking, things different in themselves are different from each other. As then nothing illustrates the philosophy of attraction more than the loveliness of woman, so is it one of the impossibilities of nature for unloveli- ness to make itself attractive. It is against every rule of common sense, common observation and the common practices of life that love and domestic tyranny should dwell together. We have no slight suspicion of our own that one great cause of domestic differences—household dissensions 'twixt man and wife, arises from the same Mrs. Caudle spirit which breathes itself like an evil odor around the family fireside. The poet Dryden has a poem upon the subject of the chief desire of woman, and he lays it down with much force of argument as well as aptness of illustration, that the *love of sway* surpasses all other feelings and propensities of the female breast. Whether universal or not, it becometh us not to say—that is does exist *sometimes* we do know, and our Sketchee, Miss Roseblossom, is the case in point.

The homage and fealty which man pays to woman, like the "quality of mercy, is not strained"—it springs forth spontaneously from the soul of the human heart. The seed that plants it is the light of the eye, the withery of the smile, and the sweet music of the voice—but if this *light* be daggers and darning-needles, this *smile* be tartness and vinegar—this *music* be the voice not of the "charmer" but of the scold, the seeds of Love will not germinate, and no tender plant of young affection can bud forth.

> "It is vain that we would coldy gaze
> On such a smile upon us; and the heart
> Leaps kindly back to kindness"

The poet speaks truly, and never, no never, hear it, ye to whom the admonition applies, and mark, learn and inwardly digest its truth, will aught but smiles, and the sweetest of them, serve to win over, and gently to lead the hearts of these stern and suborn creatures of earthly make, called men. The sharp, shrill tones of authority may *Caudleize* the souls of men, and thus render them craven-hearted and lame, but affection is all shipwrecked by the operation of certainty.

Miss Roseblossom, therefore, lives a maiden, and she will no doubt die one. The blessedness of a feminine nature is all turned into wormwood and bitterness, and instead of softness of voice, and sweetness of lips, and serenity of smiles, there dwells about the mortal physiognomy of this elderly branch of the virgin tree nothing but thorns and fish-hooks, together with "envy, hatred, malice, and all uncharitableness." The sweet milk of human kindness has long since become curdled and sour, and now there is no help for ugliness and ill-nature. We did not think to describe the person of this lady, but we are fearful the sex might consider us as slanderous—but let us not be misunderstood. We pay tribute to loveliness, and yield such homage as men are wont to feminine beauty and feminine worth; our testimony is against the opposite of these, and we have a perfect abhorrence of a sharp tongue and a tart phiz; and it is as true as the unmistakable accents of kindness that the passions and evil bitternesses of the heart do stamp themselves upon the lineaments of the face, and upon the whole outward semblance of the individual. Do we wonder then that our *tart* one—not our fair one—presented the outwardness of

> "A lizard's body, lean and long,
> A fish's head, a serpent's tongue,"

Or that the features of her face were moulded and formed upon the infernal sourness of her mind? Let me, however, rather pity than wholly condemn those unhappy frailties of human temper which so completely enslave their possessors and render them the object of popular disfavor and disregard; and let us particularly call upon those who are still lovely and still attractive, to ponder well wherein their loveliness and their attractiveness consists, so that they may not wither upon the stem as Miss Virginity Roseblossom has done.

———— + ————

Sketches of the Sidewalks and Levee; With Glimpses into the New Orleans Bar (rooms)

Ephraim Broadhorn. A Flatboatman from Kentucky

THURSDAY, AUGUST 10, 1848

Ephraim Broadhorn was bred and born, or rather, was born and bred, in the State of Connecticut. At the early age of eighteen he made tracks from the land of steady habits, and by curious train of incidents and adven-

The Jolly Flatboatmen, by George Caleb Bingham, 1846.
National Art Gallery.

tures found himself, ere he was a man fully grown, in the Commonwealth of Kentucky, where he *fraternized,* in the most harmonious manner, with a certain interesting class of sovereign people of that State, called flatboatmen. We do not suppose, on a rough guess, that betwixt the rising and the setting sun there is any people that breathe in a larger share of this same freedom than the b'hoys from "Old Kentuck." They are verily of those who

> "Love their land because it is their own,
> And scorn to give aught other reason why—
> Would shake hands with the king upon his throne,
> And think it kindness to his majesty."

Ephraim became "one of 'em," and at the age of thirty or upwards, was as unsophisticated a double specimen of Yankee and the Hoosier as ever trod the streets of Orleans in a pair of coarse brogans. It was some time during the past spring that Ephraim landed his flatboat at the Levee, and we chanced to see him as he jumped ashore. His dress was in three pieces—shirt, trowsers and straw hat: the former soiled by a fortnight's wear and tear at the oar, amid sweat and sunshine; the second was "more holy than righteous," as he himself expressed it, and his old straw hat was in keeping with the balance of his apparel. He was not only sunburnt but sunbrowned—hair and beard both lank and long, and reddened by exposure. All this, however, was but a trifle, and merely an incident to the toil which these hardy, double-fisted fellows endure while wending their way, all so tediously, and for weeks together, at the mercy of the current of the Mississippi. All these outward insignia of the "*flatboatman*" were, as we have said, trifles, which the sharp shears and sharpers razors of the barber, together with a clean muslin shirt and a bran new suit of homemade jeans, soon reformed and changed entirely. He was, in fact, a well-made, athletic man, rising six feet and upwards in height, and with a countenance as broad and open as a dinner plate.

This was Ephraim's first visit to Orleans, and being shirted and shaved, and dressed up in decent style—albeit, somewhat rustic in his apparel—he sallied forth to see the wonders of the city. To a stranger, there is nothing more striking, at first glance, in this renowned *omnium gatherum,* than the feeding propensities of its citizens: he who mixes in the walks of men, towards the baiting hour of the day, will scarcely fail to make the observation. Ephraim went with the crowd, and soon found himself planted in front of a counter covered with good things, and his "mouth fairly watered" as his eye and his appetite were both feasted upon the savory dishes before him. A very busy young man, with shirt-sleeves rolled up, and a white apron on, paid his respects to Ephraim by fixing the fingers of both hands perpendicularly upon the counter, and staring our Kentuckian directly in the face.

"What will you please to have, Sir?"

"Any thing you please," said Ephraim, "so as it's good, and don't cost too much. I s'pose you sell them ere vittles?"

"No, Sir; it's lunch—no charge for lunch—have soup?"

"Yes; I'll go it on a dish of soup," said Ephraim: and so he did, and fared sumptuously. After which he took a piece of roast beef, and a glass of brandy to wash it down, seeing the feeders on his right hand and upon his left did the same. Paying his dime like any other "high-minded, honorable fellow," and declaring it to be "darn'd cheap, considerin' it was Orleans," our raw flatboatman crammed both hands into his trowser's pockets, and stalked about the bar-room of that noted restaurant in —— street.

Indeed, it was high noon, and the congregated citizens were doing the honors of their daily lunch. We sometimes think the poet was in error, to say,

> "This life is all a fleeting show,
> For man's delusion given."

Judging from the zest with which a man enjoys himself in such a "busi-ness operation" as eating and drinking, there does seem to be some reality in it. Whatever may be a man's general feelings in regard to himself, and his rela-tions to society, he certainly loves to avail himself of that choice gift of Dame Nature, namely, a good appetite—he loves to feed: and, although in itself, this is an animal instinct, yet, when refined by friendly intercourse, it becomes a "feast of reason," as well as of beef-steak, and a flow of kindness as well as of distilled liquor. The business, we say, of lunch, for the praiseworthy purpose of staying the turbulent stomachs of men, was at this hour going on, and a long row of honest individuals were "going it." The rattling of dishes and the clanging of glasses, and the musical jingling of silver coin, were all heard, and loud rose the din thereof. The bar-keepers were busy, very busy, in the com-pounding of divers mixtures, such as are manufactured for "home consump-tion" in these grand public resorts: and the business of the "Exchange" was in a condition of progress. Why it is a coffee-house should be styled an "Exchange," as it is popularly here in New Orleans, it were hard to divine, except it be the bartering off of pocket-money for "wet damnation," as Charles Lamb curiously called that which he and most of his brother poets and essayists loved very much themselves—that is, strong drink. In the latitude or Orleans, there are but few ascetics and consequently, while the citizens thank God for the boun-ties of life, they take very good care to avail themselves of all the advantages and enjoyments accruing therefrom.

But enough on this topic lest we lose sight of our protegé and hero, Ephraim Broadhorn—a sovereign, a "dimocrat," a one of the b'hoys, all the way from old Kentuck—wandering about the streets of New Orleans "to see the elephant."

"I say, Mister," said Ephraim, stopping a Frenchman at the corner of one of the streets in the lower part of town, "I say, is this 'ere a street or is it a Rue?"

"C' est la même chose," replied Monsieur.

"It's the name of my shoes!" echoed Ephraim, mistaking the sound, and being rather raw in the language of the parlezvous—"zounds and thunder if ever I hearn tell of sich a man, I come from Kentuck, and I want to know about this 'ere road 'twixt the houses, and you tell me it's the *name of my shoes.*"

"Qu'est—ce que c'est?" asked the French gentleman in perfect surprise, as much unable to comprehend Ephraim's Kentucky dialect, as the latter was to understand accents of the Parisian vernacular.

"Kiss who, did you say?" said Ephraim. "Why, I'll be darned if I've seed any body in Orleans that a feller would want to kiss—such a variety of white humans, and black humans, and yaller humans! I wonder whar on airth they all did spring from anyhow; they must'a cotch the mud color from washin' in the Missippy river so, all their lives—don't you reckon so, Squire?"

"Aha! vous etes mystère!" cried out the other with impatience, betaking himself with accustomed rapidity down *la Rue Royale.*

"Well, I do calculate you're right for once, boss, if your mouth is all hid away thar in a bundle of whiskers and hair," said the flatboatman, standing still in the centre of the pavement and looking after the vanishing form of Monsieur; "you're right for once, my name is Mister, though its only when I get out from home and dress'd up a little, that folks put a handle to my name."

Ephraim was rather a rare chicken, we allow—rare to those not accustomed to his like. But you'll find an abundance of Ephraim Broadhorn's all through the South Western States, in Kentucky and Tennessee particularly, where they form perhaps a goodly portion of the community—sufficient to be reckoned upon as "some" on the day of the election. Rough, hardy fellows, whose frankness and good nature are equally characteristic, and whose worldly shrewdness in a small way is only surpassed by their courage and perseverance. That single line of the poet Halleck, seems to give a better idea of them than anything we can adduce:

"A stubborn race—fearing and flattering none."

To see Ephraim as he goes staring and gawking about a city, one would form an unfair estimate not only of the man, but of his class. He is out of his element here, and his appearance is coarse and his actions awkward and under constraint. We admire the plain, blunt, honest, and open character of our Western b'hoys, and although appearing to a disadvantage here in town, where fashion reigns and where the artificial predominates, yet

—"View them near
At home, where all their worth and pride is placed:
And there their hospitable fires burn clear,
And there the lowliest farm-house hearth is graced
With manly hearts."

To talk about their intelligence, in the sense of learning, as is common with political demagogues, is all stuff; but they possess what answers an excellent purpose in the matter of pure republicanism and which William Pinckney, many years ago, avowed to be his main reliance—namely: "the unsophisticated good sense and noble spirit of the American people."

EPILOGUE

Memories of New Orleans

———— ✦ ————

Manuscript Fragment about New Orleans

(ca. 1848, with Later Additions)

March 18th. We have now been publishing "the *Crescent*," two weeks; and it seems to be going ahead handsomely. My situation is rather a pleasant one. I get through at evening much earlier than I had anticipated, which I like, of course, very well. There are many peculiarities in New Orleans that I shall jot down at my leisure in these pages. It seems somewhat strange that I have not heard from home. It is now over a month, and no letter yet.

(I arrived in New Orleans, on the night of Friday Feb. 25th; and left it Saturday afternoon, May 27th, '48.)

On board steamer *Griffith* Upper part of Lake Huron, Saturday morning, June 10th, 1848.

For a few weeks after I commenced my duties at New Orleans, matters went on very pleasantly. People seemed to treat me kindly, particularly H. and M'C. My health was most capital; I frequently thought indeed that I felt better than ever before in my life. After changing my boarding house, Jef. and I were, take it altogether, pretty comfortable. We had good beds, and though the noise was incessant, day and night, we slept well. The plan of going to dinner when we liked, and calling for what we wanted, out of a variety of dishes, was more convenient than the usual way of boarding houses.

Through some unaccountable means, however, both H. and M'C, after a while, exhibited a singular sort of coldness, toward me, and the latter an irritability toward Jef., who had, at times, much harder work than I was willing he should do.

The arrangements of the office were in this wise: I generally went about my work about 9 o'clock, overhauling the papers rec'd by mail, and "making up the news," as it is called, both with pen and scissors. A Mr. Larue (a good writer,) generally prepared the leading editorials; Mr. Reeder, (an amiable-hearted young man, but excessively intemperate) was the "city news" man; (poor Reeder is dead, since) and a young fellow named DaPonte, officiated as translator of Mexican and foreign news items; factotum in general. I had been accustomed to having frequent conferences, in my former situations with the proprietors of newspapers, on the subject of management, etc. But when the coldness above alluded to broke out, H. seemed to be studiously silent upon all these matters. My own pride was touched—and I met their conduct with equal haughtiness on my part. On Wednesday May 24th I sent down a note requesting a small sum of money. M'C returned me a bill of what money I had already drawn, and stated that they could not make "advances." I answered by reminding them of certain points which appeared to have been forgotten, making me not their debtor, and told them in my reply I thought it would be better to dissolve the connection. They agreed to my plan (after some objections on the part of me); and I determined to leave on the succeeding Saturday.

Accordingly on Friday I packed up my traps. . . .

———— + ————

New Orleans in 1848

(*New Orleans Picayune,* January 25, 1887)

Walt Whitman gossips of his sojourn here years ago as a newspaper writer. Notes of his trip up the Mississippi and to New York.

Among the letters brought this morning (Camden, New Jersey, Jan. 15, 1887,) by my faithful post-office carrier, J.G., is one as follows:

"NEW ORLEANS, Jan. 11, '87.—We have been informed that when you were younger and less famous than now, you were in New Orleans and perhaps have helped on the *Picayune*. If you have any remembrance of the *Picayune's* young days, or of journalism in New Orleans of that era, and would put it in writing (verse or prose) for the *Picayune's* fiftieth year edition, Jan. 25, we shall be pleased," etc.

In response to which: I went down to New Orleans early in 1848 to work on a daily newspaper, but it was not the *Picayune,* though I saw quite a good deal of the editors of that paper, and knew its personnel and ways. But let me indulge my pen in some gossipy recollections of that time and place, with extracts from my journal up the Mississippi and across the great lakes to the Hudson.

Probably the influence most deeply pervading everything at that time through the United States, both in physical facts and in sentiment, was the Mexican War, then just ended. Following a brilliant campaign (in which our troops had march'd to the capital city, Mexico, and taken full possession,) we were returning after our victory. From the situation of the country, the city of New Orleans had been our channel and *entrepot* for everything, going and returning. It had the best news and war correspondents; it had the most to say, through its leading papers, the *Picayune* and *Delta* especially, and its voice was readiest listen'd to; from it "Chapparal" had gone out, and his army and battle letters were copied everywhere, not only in the United States, but in Europe. Then the social cast and results; no one who has never seen the society of a city under similar circumstances can understand what a strange vivacity and *rattle* were given throughout by such a situation. I remember the crowds of soldiers, the gay young officers, going or coming, the receipt of important news, the many discussions, the returning wounded, and so on.

I remember very well seeing Gen. Taylor with his staff and other officers at the St. Charles Theatre one evening (after talking with them during the day.) There was a short play on the stage, but the principal performance was of Dr. Collyer's troupe of "Model Artists," then in the full tide of their popularity. They gave many fine groups and solo shows. The house was crowded with uniforms and shoulder-straps. Gen. T. himself, if I remember right, was almost the only officer in civilian clothes; he was a jovial, old, rather stout, plain man, with a wrinkled and dark-yellow face, and, in ways and manners, show'd the least of conventional ceremony or etiquette I ever saw; he laugh'd unrestrainedly at everything comical. (He had a great personal resemblance to Fenimore Cooper, the novelist, of New York.) I remember Gen. Pillow and quite a cluster of other militaires also present.

One of my choice amusements during my stay in New Orleans was going down to the old French Market, especially of a Sunday morning. The show was a varied and curious one; among the rest, the Indian and negro hucksters with their wares. For there were always fine specimens of Indians, both men and women, young and old. I remember I nearly always on these occasions got a large cup of delicious coffee with a biscuit, for my breakfast, from the immense shining copper kettle of a great Creole mulatto woman (I believe she weigh'd 230 pounds.) I never have had such coffee since. About nice drinks, anyhow, my recollection of the "cobblers" (with strawberries and snow on top of the large tumblers,) and also the exquisite wines, and the perfect and mild French brandy, help the regretful reminiscence of my New Orleans experiences of those days. And what splendid and roomy and leisurely bar-rooms! particularly the grand ones of the St. Charles and St. Louis. Bargains, auctions, appointments, business conferences, &c., were generally held in the spaces or recesses of these bar-rooms.

I used to wander a midday hour or two now and then for amusement on the crowded and bustling levees, on the banks of the river. The diagonally wedg'd-in boats, the stevedores, the piles of cotton and other merchandise, the carts, mules, negroes, etc., afforded never-ending studies and sights to me. I made acquaintances among the captains, boatmen, or other characters, and often had long talks with them—sometimes finding a real rough diamond among my chance encounters. Sundays I sometimes went forenoons to the old Catholic Cathedral in the French quarter. I used to walk a good deal in this arrondissement; and I have deeply regretted since that I did not cultivate, while I had such a good opportunity, the chance of better knowledge of French and Spanish Creole New Orleans people. (I have an idea that there is much and of importance about the Latin race contributions to American nationality in the South and Southwest that will never be put with sympathetic understanding and tact on record.)

Let me say, for better detail, that through several months (1848) I work'd on a new daily paper, *The Crescent;* my situation rather a pleasant one. My young brother, Jeff, was with me; and he not only grew very homesick, but the climate of the place, and especially the water, seriously disagreed with him. From this and other reasons (although I was quite happily fix'd) I made no very long stay in the South. In due time we took passage northward for St. Louis in the "Pride of the West" steamer, which left her wharf just at dusk. My brother was unwell, and lay in his berth from the moment we left till the next morning; he seem'd to me to be in a fever, and I felt alarm'd. However, the next morning he was all right again, much to my relief.

Our voyage up the Mississippi was after the same sort as the voyage, some months before, down it. The shores of this great river are very monotonous and dull—one continuous and rank flat, with the exception of a meagre stretch of bluff, about the neighborhood of Natchez, Memphis, &c. Fortunately we had good weather, and not a great crowd of passengers, though the berths were all full. The "Pride" jogg'd along pretty well, and put us into St. Louis about noon Saturday. After looking around a little I secured passage on the steamer "Prairie Bird," (to leave late in the afternoon,) bound up the Illinois river to La Salle, where we were to take canal for Chicago. During the day I rambled with my brother over a large portion of the town, search'd after a refectory, and, after much trouble, succeeded in getting some dinner.

Our "Prairie Bird" started out at dark, and a couple of hours after there was quite a rain and blow, which made them haul in along shore and tie fast. We made but thirty miles the whole night. The boat was excessively crowded with passengers, and had withal so much freight that we could hardly turn around. I slept on the floor, and the night was uncomfortable enough. The Illinois river is spotted with little villages with big names, Marseilles, Naples, etc.; its banks are low, and the vegetation excessively rank. Peoria, some distance up, is a pleasant town; I went over the place; the country back is all rich land, for sale cheap. Three or four miles from P., land of the first quality can be bought for $3 or $4 an acre. (I am transcribing from my notes written at the time.)

Arriving at La Salle Tuesday morning, we went on board a canal-boat, had a detention by sticking on a mud bar, and then jogg'd along at a slow trot, some seventy of us, on a moderate-sized boat. (If the weather hadn't been rather cool, particularly at night, it would have been insufferable.) Illinois is the most splendid agricultural country I ever saw; the land is of surpassing richness; the place par excellence for farmers. We stopt at various points along the canal, some of them pretty villages.

It was 10 o'clock A.M. when we got in Chicago, too late for the steamer; so we went to an excellent public house, the "American Temperance," and I spent the time that day and till next morning, looking around Chicago.

At 9 the next forenoon we started on the "Griffith" (on board of which I am now inditing these memoranda,) up the blue waters of Lake Michigan. I was delighted with the appearance of the towns along Wisconsin. At Milwaukee I went on shore, and walk'd around the place. They say the country back is beautiful and rich. (It seems to me that if we should ever remove from Long Island, Wisconsin would be the proper place to come to.) The towns have a remarkable appearance of good living, without any penury or want. The country is so good naturally, and labor is in such demand.

About 5 o'clock one afternoon I heard the cry of "a woman over-board." It proved to be a crazy lady, who had become so from the loss of her son a couple of weeks before. The small boat put off, and succeeded in picking her up, though she had been in the water 15 minutes. She was dead. Her husband was on board. They went off at the next stopping place. While she lay in the water she probably recover'd her reason, as she toss'd up her arms and lifted her face toward the boat.

Sunday Morning, June 11.—We pass'd down Lake Huron yesterday and last night, and between 4 and 5 o'clock this morning we ran on the "flats," and have been vainly trying, with the aid of a steam tug and a lumbering lighter, to get clear again. The day is beautiful and the water clear and calm. Night before last we stopt at Mackinaw, (the island and town,) and I went up on the old fort, one of the oldest stations in the Northwest. We expect to get to Buffalo by to-morrow. The tug has fasten'd lines to us, but some have been snapt and the others have no effect. We seem to be firmly imbedded in the sand. (With the exception of a larger boat and better accommodations, it amounts to about the same thing as a becalmment I underwent on the Montauk voyage, East Long Island, last summer.) *Later.*—We are off again—expect to reach Detroit before dinner.

We did not stop at Detroit. We are now on Lake Erie, jogging along at a good round pace. A couple of hours since we were on the river above. Detroit seem'd to me a pretty place and thrifty. I especially liked the looks of the Canadian shore opposite and of the little village of Windsor, and, indeed, all along the banks of the river. From the shrubbery and the neat appearance of some of the cottages, I think it must have been settled by the French. While I now write we can see a little distance ahead the scene of the battle between Perry's fleet and the British during the last war with England. The lake looks to me a fine sheet of water. We are having a beautiful day.

June 12.—We stopt last evening at Cleveland, and though it was dark, I took the opportunity of rambling about the place; went up in the heart of the city and back to what appear'd to be the courthouse. The streets are unusually wide, and the buildings appear to be substantial and comfortable. We went down through Main street and found, some distance along, several squares of ground very prettily planted with trees and looking attractive enough. Return'd to the boat by way of the lighthouse on the hill.

This morning we are making for Buffalo, being, I imagine, a little more than half across Lake Erie. The water is rougher than on Michigan or Huron. (On St. Clair it was smooth as glass.) The day is bright and dry, with a stiff head wind.

We arriv'd in Buffalo on Monday evening; spent that night and a portion of next day going round the city exploring. Then got in the cars and went to Niagara; went under the falls—saw the whirlpool and all the other sights.

Tuesday night started for Albany; travel'd all night. From the time daylight afforded us a view of the country all seem'd very rich and well cultivated. Every few miles were large towns or villages.

Wednesday late we arriv'd at Albany. Spent the evening in exploring. There was a political meeting (Hunker) at the capitol, but I pass'd it by. Next morning I started down the Hudson in the "Alida"; arriv'd safely in New York that evening.

——— + ———

Calamus Leaves

(Manuscript)

The following is a transcription of the controversial "Calamus Leaves" manuscripts from the University of Virginia's Valentine-Barrett Collection, of a draft poem containing echoes of Whitman's experiences in New Orleans. It is more commonly known by the title "Live Oak, with Moss." It remained unpublished during Whitman's lifetime, but the majority of the text found its way into other groupings and poems in the 1860 edition of *Leaves of Grass.* The transcription is largely courtesy of the Walt Whitman Archive, though some minor adjustments to formatting have been made for readability (deletions excised, line breaks adjusted).

I.

Not the heat flames up and consumes,

Not the sea-waves hurry in and out,

Not the air, delicious and dry, the air of the ripe summer, bears lightly along white down-balls of myriads of seeds, wafted, sailing gracefully, to drop where they may,

Not these—O none of these, more than the flames of me, consuming, burning for his love whom I love—O none, more than I, hurrying in and out;

Does the tide hurry, seeking something, and never give up?—O I, the same, to seek my life-long lover;

O nor down-balls, nor perfumes, nor the high rain-emitting clouds, are borne through the open air, more than my copious soul is borne through the open air, wafted in all directions, for friendship, for love.

II.

I saw in Louisiana a live-oak growing,

All alone stood it, and the moss hung down from the branches,

Without any companion it grew there, glistening out with joyous leaves of dark green,

And its look, rude, unbending, lusty, made me think of myself;

But I wondered how it could utter joyous leaves, standing alone there without its friend, its lover—For I knew I could not;

And I plucked a twig with a certain number of leaves upon it, and twined around it a little moss, and brought it away—And I have placed it in sight in my room.

It is not needed to remind me as of my friends, (for I believe lately I think of little else than of them,)

Yet it remains to me a curious token—it makes me think of manly love;

For all that, and though the live oak glistens there in Louisiana, solitary in a wide flat space, uttering joyous leaves all its life, without a friend, a lover, near—I know very well I could not.

III.

When I heard at the close of the day how I had been praised in the Capitol, still it was not a happy night for me that followed;

Nor when I caroused—Nor when my favorite plans were accomplished—was I really happy,

But that day I rose at dawn from the bed of perfect health, electric, inhaling sweet breath,

When I saw the full moon in the west grow pale and disappear in the morning light,

When I wandered alone over the beach, and undressing, bathed, laughing with the waters, and saw the sun rise,

And when I thought how my friend, my lover, was coming, then O I was happy;

Each breath tasted sweeter—and all that day my food nourished me—And the beautiful day passed well,

And the next came with equal joy—And with the next, at evening, came my friend,

And that night, while all was still, I heard the waters roll slowly continually up the shores

I heard the hissing rustle of the liquid and sands, as directed to me, whispering, to congratulate me,—For the friend I love lay sleeping by my side,

In the stillness his face was inclined towards me, while the moon's clear beams shone, And his arm lay lightly over my breast—And that night I was happy.

And that night O you happy waters, I heard you beating the shores—But my heart beat happier than you—for he I love is returned and sleeping by my side,

And that night in the stillness his face was inclined toward me while the moon's clear beams shone,

And his arm lay lightly over my breast—And that night I was happy.

+ + +

IV.

This moment as I sit alone, yearning and pensive, it seems to me there are other men, in other lands, yearning and pensive.

It seems to me I can look over and behold them, in Germany, France, Spain—Or far away in China, India, or in Russia—talking other dialects,

And it seems to me if I could know those men, I should love them as I love men in my own lands;

It seems to me they are as wise, beautiful, benevolent, as any in my own lands;

O I think we should be brethren—I think I should be happy with them.

V.

Long I thought that knowledge alone would suffice me—O if I could but obtain knowledge!

Then the Land of the Prairies engrossed me—the south savannas engrossed me—For them I would live—I would be their orator;

Then I met the examples of old and new heroes—I heard of warriors, sailors, and all dauntless persons—And it seemed to me I too had it in me to be as dauntless as any, and would be so;

And then to finish all, it came to me to strike up the songs of the New World— And then I believed my life must be spent in singing;

But now take notice, Land of the prairies, Land of the south savannas, Ohio's land,

Take notice, you Kanuck woods—and you, Lake Huron—and all that with you roll toward Niagara—and you Niagara also,

And you, Californian mountains—that you all find some one else that he be your singer of songs,

For I can be your singer of songs no longer—I have ceased to enjoy them.

I have found him who loves me, as I him in perfect love,

With the rest I dispense—I sever from all that I thought would suffice me, for it does—it is now empty and tasteless to me,

I heed knowledge, and the grandeur of The States, and the examples of heroes, no more,

I am indifferent to my own songs—I am to go with him I love, and he is to go with me,

It is to be enough for each of us that we are together—We never separate again.

VI.

What think you I have taken my pen to record?

Not the battle-ship, perfect-model'd, majestic, that I saw to day arrive in the offing, under full sail,

Nor the splendors of the past day—nor the splendors of the night that envelopes me—Nor the glory and growth of the great city spread around me,

But the two young men I saw to-day on the pier, parting the parting of dear friends.

The one to remain hung on the other's neck and passionately kissed him—while the one to depart tightly prest the one to remain in his arms.

VII.

You bards of ages hence! when you refer to me, mind not so much my poems,

Nor speak to me that I prophesied of The States and led them the way of their glories,

But come, I will inform you who I was underneath that impassive exterior—I will tell you what to say of me,

Publish my name and hang up my picture as that of the tenderest lover,

The friend, the lover's portrait, of whom his friend, his lover was fondest,

Who was not proud of his songs, but of the measureless ocean of love within him—and freely poured it forth,

Who often walked lonesome walks thinking of his dearest friends, his lovers,

Who pensive, away from one he loved, often lay sleepless and dissatisfied at night,

Who, dreading lest the one he loved might after all be indifferent to him, felt the sick feeling—O sick! sick!

Whose happiest days were those, far away through fields, in woods, on hills, he and another, wandering hand in hand, they twain, apart from other men.

Who ever, as he sauntered the streets, curved with his arm the manly shoulder of his friend—while the curving arm of his friend rested upon him also.

VIII.

Hours continuing long, sore and heavy-hearted,

Hours of the dusk, when I withdraw to a lonesome and unfrequented spot, seating myself, leaning my face in my hands,

Hours sleepless, deep in the night, when I go forth, speeding swiftly the country roads, or through the city streets, or pacing miles and miles, stifling plaintive cries,

Hours discouraged, distracted,—For he, the one I cannot content myself without—soon I saw him content himself without me,

Hours when I am forgotten—(O weeks and months are passing, but I believe I am never to forget!)

Sullen and suffering hours—(I am ashamed—but it is useless—I am what I am;)

Hours of my torment—I wonder if other men ever have the like out of the like feelings?

Is there even one other like me—distracted—his friend, his lover, lost to him?

Is he too as I am now? Does he still rise in the morning, dejected, thinking who is lost to him? And at night, awaking, think who is lost?

Does he too harbor his friendship silent and endless? Harbor his anguish and passion?

Does some stray reminder, or the casual mention of a name, bring the fit back upon him, taciturn and deprest?

Does he see himself reflected in me? In these hours does he see the face of his hours reflected?

IX.

I dreamed in a dream of a city where all the men were like brothers,

O I saw them tenderly love each other—I often saw them, in numbers, walking hand in hand;

I dreamed that was the city of robust friends—Nothing was greater there than manly love—it led the rest,

It was seen every hour in the actions of the men of that city, and in all their looks and words.

X.

O you whom I often and silently come where I you are, that I may be with you,

As I walk by your side, or sit near, or remain in the same room with you,

Little you know the subtle electric fire that for your sake is playing within me.

XI.

Earth! Though you look so impassive, ample and spheric there—I now suspect
    that is not all,
I now suspect there is something terrible in you, ready to break forth,
For an athlete loves me, and I him—But toward him there is something fierce
    and terrible in me,
I dare not tell it in words—not even in these songs.

XII.

To the young man, many things to absorb, to engraft, to develop, I teach, that
    he be my eleve,
But if through him speed not the blood of friendship, hot and red—If he be not
    silently selected by lovers, and do not silently select lovers—of what use
    were it for him to seek to become eleve of mine?

APPENDIX A

Letters from Thomas Jefferson ("Jeff") Whitman to His Family

These letters are reproduced courtesy of the Walt Whitman Archive. Jeff was fourteen at the time of composition and had limited schooling by today's standards. His often highly idiosyncratic spelling and grammar have been corrected for the sake of readability. Some passages not directly related to the volume at hand have been excised. Full, uncorrected versions of these documents can be accessed in the Correspondence section of the Whitman Archive.

---- ✦ ----

Mid–February: Trip to New Orleans and First Impressions

... Our captain thought he would run the risk and save the time (it takes some time longer to go through the canal) so he got a flat-boat and took out some of the freight, and we started to go over the falls. Father can judge how fast we went, when I tell him it is a fall of twenty feet, within a space of three miles. And what is most dangerous, the bottom is covered with very large rock which leave a very small channel for the boat. When you get about the middle there is a large rock in this channel, and one on each side of it, the one on the right side is a little distance from the one in the middle, just room enough for a boat to pass through. So you have to take a very sudden turn, or the boat is smashed all to pieces. It happened that we got off with a little bump on each rock, we should not have got that (for we had the best pilots that could be found) but one wheel would not work. The fun of the whole thing was the *fright* we all had. Some of the passengers went to bed, others walked the cabin floor, looking as gloomy as if they were going to be hung. Although I was frightened a good deal, it was not so much as some of the *men* were. If the boat had sunk, we would have been within a few feet of the shore, but I don't think we could have got there, the current was so swift.

Mother, you have no idea of the splendor and the comfort of these western river steam-boats. The cabin is on the deck, and state rooms on each side of it, there are two beds in each room. The greatest of all these splendors is the eating department (you know I always did love eating). Every thing you would find in the Astor house in New York, you find on these boats.

I will give you a little description of the way we live on board. For breakfast we have: coffee, tea, ham and eggs, beef steak, sausages hot cakes, with plenty of good bread, sugar, &c, &c. For dinner: roast beef mutton, veal, boiled ham, roast turkey, goose with pie, and puddings, and for supper every thing that is good to eat. . . .

Saturday noon. Last night we had a very hard storm, it rained hard and blew harder. We expect to get as far as Cairo to-night on the Mississippi River. Nothing of importance has occurred since yesterday.

Sunday night. We have arrived at last, at New Orleans. We came in on Friday night about ten o'clock.

Saturday, Walter found a board in Poydras St, corner St Charles. You must direct your letters thusly: Walter Whitman, New Orleans, La. Saturday was a drizzly rainy day. I hope they don't have many of them

Monday, yesterday, was quite warm. I saw a good many peach trees in blossom to-day. Walter will get the first number of his out on Sunday next.

Dear Mother, I must bid you good-bye for a little while. I will write to you again pretty soon. Dear Father, I will write to you also pretty soon until then good-bye, one and all.

Jefferson Whitman

Dear Mother, write often

✦ ✦ ✦

———— ✦ ————

March 14: Employment at the *Crescent* and City Perambulations

Dear Father,

since I wrote to Mother nothing of importance has transpired. This will be the eighth or ninth letter we have sent you, and we have not received a single one from you. Mr. Wilson in the *Eagle* office sent Walter one in which he said that he called there and that you were all well. Do write to us, Father, even half a sheet would be better than nothing. I go to the post office every day so we shall get it as soon as it gets here. . . .

Walter and myself are very well. I am now at work in the "Crescent" office at *five* dollars per week, and my work is done by three o'clock every afternoon. I don't know how long I shall stay there, but it shall be as long as I can make it.

Walter gets home much sooner than he thought he should; he is hardly ever later than eleven o'clock, and one night he was home at half past nine o'clock, he gets a few books most every day but none of them worth much.

Father, you wanted me to ask how much carpenter's wages were here. I am told they are from forty to fifty dollars a month, which I think is a pretty good sum, but every-thing is so much here that you hardly know whether you get a good bargain or not.

To My Dear Mother:

I do want to hear from you very, very much, do write to Walter or me and tell us how you have been getting along since we came away and give a description of sister Mary's visit (I wrote her a letter soon after we got here). I will give you a little bit of city news.

New Orleans is a very level place and you do not dig down more than two feet before you come to the water. It is also a very dirty place. Mother, I never wanted your cleanliness so much before as I did at our first boarding house. You could not only see the dirt, but you could taste it, and you had to, too, if you ate anything at all. And the rooms, too, were covered with dirt an inch thick. But now we are through with all that. We are now living at the Tremont house, next door to the Theatre and directly opposite the office.

There have been two or three processions (and one thing or other) days since we have been here, and some rather funny ones, too. [. . .]

Last Sunday we took a walk in the old Catholic cemetery, and a very beautiful place it is, too. Flowers of every description were on some of the tombs, large white roses and red ones too were all along the walk from one end to the other. At night, too, the streets are filled with women with baskets full of flowers.

On Sunday morning, we took a walk down to the old French church and an old-looking thing it is, too. Every one would go up and dip their fingers in the holy water and then go home and *whip* their *slaves*. One old black took a bottle full home to wash the sins out of her family.

I will write to you Mother again; you must write to me as often as you possibly can.

To George and Andrew.

Dear Brothers, I should like to see you very much but, as I cannot, you must write to me, too. On Saturday the 4th of March we had a grand fireman's procession and I think it was larger than the one (the firemen part) in New York. The engines were very large and were drawn by horses (six or eight). Right opposite of here, they are fixing it up for a balloon ascension on next Sunday. I suppose I shall see all the fun. I am going to night to see Mr. Collins and I expect some fun. You must write to me as soon as you can.

To Sister Hannah.

Dear Sister. Your part of the letter comes on the part where there are no lines, so I think it will be pretty crooked, but you must not mind that. I believe I promised to send you something but every thing is so d—— much that I cannot get it.

New Orleans would be just the place for you. You could have flowers all the year round, which I know you are a great lover of. By the bye, Walter wants to know (and you must tell him in your letter) whether the trees and flowers he sat out are living yet. Dear Sister, you must also write to me (but please pay the postage). Among the others I must not forget my dear brother.

Eddy you must go to school and try to write and read so I can send letters to you and you can read them.

I must bid you all good-bye. but I will write again soon.

Good-bye Father, good-bye Mother, good-bye all

Jefferson Whitman

———— ✦ ————

March 27: Daily Life

Dear Mother

To-day we received the first letter from you, and glad enough we were to get it, too. [. . .] You say the weather is very cold there; here it is just the other way. That is, it is pretty warm. I have now begun to wear the summer clothes sister Hannah made me which I find very comfortable. . . .

You need not be alarmed about the yellow fever as that gentleman will (the folks think) not visit this place this summer. The reason they give for that is this. It does not come but once in three or four years, and last season it was very hard and killed a great many persons (I mean it does not come but once in three or four years in such a shape). Besides it is a great humbug, most every one in our office has had it (some of them have had it twice) and got well. It is caused mostly (I think all of it) by the habits of the people, they never meet a friend, but you have to go drink and such loose habits. You know that Walter is averse to such habits, so you need not be afraid of our taking it.

Yesterday, we were to have a balloon ascension, but just as it was ready to go up the balloon busted, so it did not go up. This is the third time she (it was a lady that was to go up in it) has tried it and each time failed.

We are very nicely situated in our new place;—just "around the corner" is a very fine public park, which we take a walk in every night

I believe I told you in my last letter that I was also at work at the "Crescent" office at five dollars a week, and I have the exchange papers for which I get twenty five cents per hundred, in a few weeks I expect to get two dollars a week for them.

If you do not get the paper (the "Crescent") regularly you must send Andrew or George down to the Eagle office for it, I always see that two copies go every morning. My work is good and light. I have such a part of the mail (and I can do it most over night) and then I have nothing to do for the rest of the day (I generally get through with it about two o'clock) but stay in the office.

We have (I think) got along very well for such a long journey, not a single accident occurred on the way

Dear Father, I hope you are getting along good with your work &c. Mother says it is cold so you can't work here it is warm enough. In building houses here, they do not do as they do in New York. Here, they dig a hole in the ground some two feet deep and about the same width, and in length as far as the wall is to go, (they cannot dig cellars here like in the north. You don't dig in the ground more than two feet before it is filled with water.) This trench they cover the bottom with boards (the ground is mostly made of quick-sand) and then build the wall on it. They cannot make good brick here, so they have to come from a distance. Carpenters wages are very high here, some forty to fifty dollars a month and found.

I will write a letter to you pretty soon, but in this one I must not forget George's and Andrew's.

Dear brothers, I should like to see you very much indeed, but I suppose I cannot, you must make Mother or Hannah write to us as often as they can. There is nothing, I believe, there is not anything here you would like to hear from or of.

Dear Sister, I should like to see you very much indeed, but I suppose you would like to hear about the ladies in N.O. They are something like the "critters" in N.Y. except they were one or two more "flounces" and live more in the open air, &c, &c, &c, &c, &c, &c.

To Eddy. You must go to school and learn to read and write and then you must send letters to me, besides you must be a good boy, &c.

And now Dear Mother I must bid you good-bye for a little while but will write to you again shortly.

We are both very well and the warm air agrees with Walter very much. I have had a little attack of the dysentery, but I am very, very well now. In fact, I have not been sick much at all.

Dear Mother, good-bye

your son Jefferson Whitman.

My best respects to the rest of the family.

——— ✦ ———

April 23: Sickness and Home-Sickness

Dear Parents,

Since I wrote to you (the night after we got your only letter) we have heard nothing from you. It is very strange you do not write oftener to us, for we have written to you ever so many times. Now we have been from home nearly three months, and we have received only one letter from you. I beg of you to write to us often . . .

Walter is very well; indeed, he thinks this place agrees with him very much and he says he feels better than ever he did in New York. And I to feel pretty well but not so much so as I intend to be. I have still a kind of summer complaint, which does not feel very good, but it is very far from being really sick[. . . .]

Walter is trying to save up all the money he can get, and already he has quite a sum. As soon as he gets a thousand dollars he is coming north. And I, too, am saving all I can get. I give Walter five dollars (my wages) every week, and I have sold about five dollars' worth of old papers. That, you know, is all clear gain, all the trouble it is, is to count them out and put them up in hundreds.

Yesterday evening and this morning is the finest weather we have had since we have been here. Just warm and just cool enough to make it very pleasant. We took a very long walk last night, way out Camp street beyond the limits of the city. There are no hills like on old Long Island. The whole state is as level as a race course. In some of the streets they have a kind of canal or drain to let the water run off, and even then, in some places there is not enough "down-hill" to make it run off good. Just a little farther up town there is a canal (of a larger kind than those in the middle of the street) where sloops, &c., can come up from the lake (about 7 miles westward of the city). Along by this canal (the "new canal," they call it) there is a road called shell road where we take frequent (and very pleasant) walks, the road is nearly as hard as a brick, and on a pleasant afternoon is covered with carriages of every description. It seems to be the fashion to drive your horse as fast as he can go.

The price of a good apple here (such a one as you could get in New York for a cent and at some places two for a cent) is the small price of ten cents.

Sometimes, I get thinking about you all and feel quite lonesome, but not one fifth as much as I did when we first arrived here. At first, I could not make myself believe that we were so far away from home, but it is something of a distance[. . . .]

You will remember that I said that we were to have a balloon ascension opposite our boarding house, the thing was tried four or five times, but as just enough persons got inside the thing would manage to burst. A few Sundays ago, it was said it would go up again, they had got it all ready when it blew all to pieces. The persons that had paid to see it thought it was nothing but a suck in (which I think was the case). As soon as it touched the ground, they all laid hold of it, and dragging it over the fence tore it all to pieces, they did not leave a piece a foot square. So ended all that

Monday April 24th . . .

To-day has been a very fine clear day, the ladies were out in great numbers. The city has been very lively to-day.

Mother. Just think what you would think of us, if we had written you only one letter since we came away. I am afraid you would think pretty hard of us. Father and Hannah need a little "blowing up" too, but I will generously let them off, if they will promise to write often in future.

I have almost filled the whole sheet out so I must stop. I shall write to you again pretty soon, until then good-bye.

                                        your son Jefferson Whitman [. . .]

APPENDIX B

Additional Editorials

———— ✦ ————

Model Artists
MONDAY, MARCH 6, 1848

Half the newspapers we get from the North have something to say about the "Model Artists"; often in a tone of very severe condemnation. They say the sight of such things is indecent; if that be so, the sight of nearly all the great works of painting and sculpture—pronounced by the united voice of critics of all nations to be master-pieces of genius—is, likewise, indecent. It is a sickly prudishness that beholds only the indelicacy of such things—a prudishness that bars all appreciation of the divine beauty evidenced in Nature's cunningest work—the human frame, form and face.

There may be some petty attempts, in the low by-places, which all cities have, to counterfeit these groupings, after a vile method. Such, however, are only to be seen by those who go specially to see them. Of the graceful and beautiful groupings—most of them after models in sculpture—exhibited by persons of taste and tact, it is hard to see what harm can be said.

———— ✦ ————

General Taylor at the Theatre
TUESDAY, MAY 9, 1848

Quite a sensation was created in the St. Charles Theatre, last night, by appearance of Maj. Gens. Taylor and Pillow, with some other officers of note, in the dress circle. It was just as the model artists, on the stage, were in the midst of their tableau of the "Circassian Slaves," that the hero of Buena Vista, and his companions, entered the house. In the dim light, the gas being turned off to give effect to the performances, the General's entrance was not noticed by the audience. When the lights shone out again, however, the most vociferous cheering announced that the people recognized him. The orchestra played "The Star-spangled Banner" and "Hail Columbia"—and the next tableau was one purposely complimentary to Gen. Taylor. It was received with loud cheering and plaudits.

——— ✦ ———

A Question of Propriety
TUESDAY, MARCH 14, 1848

Our contemporary of the Mobile *Herald* disagrees altogether from some humble remarks of ours, last week, on the subject of "Model Artists"— and, (as near as we remember, for the paper containing the remarks alluded to has been mislaid,) disagrees also from our opinion of the perfect propriety of sculptures and paintings after a similar sort with these "Artists." In what we said, and in what we have to say, it is not so much about the Model Artists, but the general principle involved, that we care. Much has been written on the subject of that principle in this country; for among the nations on the continent of Europe it has been settled long ago, A portion of the English hold out still; but they do it more from the proverbial obstinacy of John Bull, than from any other reason.

The only objection that we conceive of to the undraped figure, arises from an assumption of coarseness and grossness intended. Take away this, and there is no need (in the cases under discussion) of any objection at all. Eve in Paradise—or Adam either—would not be supposed to shock the mind. Neither would the sight of those inhabitants of the Pacific Islands, whose nakedness is, or was, the innocent and usual custom. Neither does the sight of youth, among us or any where else. And, so stern and commanding is the potency of genius, even over the vulgar—neither do copies of the Venus de Medicia; for the prude dare not open his mouth against what the world, for many a year, has pronounced divine. It is only when people *will* try hard to think exclusively of what they assume to be a grossness intended, that they are "shocked" at such spectacles. But would not a woman of sense, (to say nothing of a man of sense, whose delicacies are not supposed to be so super-refined,) even if her education has been rigid in this respect, do better to take it for granted that *no* grossness is intended? Is there any absolute need of directing the mind the worser way?

Amid all the works of that Power which, in the most stupendous systems and the smallest objects in them, shows such unspeakable harmony and perfection, nothing can compare with the *human* master-piece, his closing and crowning work! It is a master-piece in *itself,* not as it is furbelowed off by the milliner and tailor. Nor would it be altogether uninteresting to pursue the inquiry how far artificial ideas on the subject of swaddling this work, so much in vogue among civilized nations—and barring off the contemplation of its noble and beautiful proportions—how far, we say, these practices may have aided in the effect of diminishing the average amplitude and majesty of the form, which effect must be confessed to when comparing present times with the age of the old Grecians and Latins.

As for the Model Artists, we know excellent women, and men, too, who have attended their performances with rational gratification. We have witnessed them with the like result. It is somewhat a matter of taste, however; and we do not wish to quarrel with any body because his taste differs from ours. In conclusion, it may be as well to state that there are perhaps, in byeplaces, exaggerated exhibitions of these groupings—as gluttony or drunkenness is the depravity of a wholesome appetite. Such, from what we hear, are so abominable as to be beneath even the merit of condemnation.

———— + ————

University Studies

TUESDAY, APRIL II, 1848

Within the last few days the attention of the public has been several times called to the course of studies now pursued or about to be pursued in the University of the State; and as few subjects can be more important to the citizens of Louisiana, it becomes us to consider the matter in the spirit of an enlarged philosophy, entirely free from the prejudices of party, and sincerely desirous of arriving at a knowledge of the means by which the wisdom and virtue of the people may be permanently increased.

Fertile as the age has been in plans for the improvement of individual and social life, in no department has the human intellect been more active than in devising systems of education, fitted both for the Common School and the University. Yet, diverse as have been the schemes proposed for training the race for its duties and its pleasures, all have admitted the general principle that the object of education is rather that of developing, strengthening and directing the faculties with which nature has endowed us, than that of imparting positive knowledge, filling the mind with a heap of disjointed facts, or making it a store-house for the reception of the exploded theories of past generations. To expand and purify the soul by the contemplation of virtue, to strengthen the mind for the search after truth, and fill it with the earnest determination of resting satisfied with no other object of pursuit, should be the primary aim of all educational means. Let it not be supposed that this need be the basis of Common School instruction only; and that as soon as the youth enters the University, the sole thing necessary is to impart a certain amount of classical lore or mathematical analysis or professional information. Were this the whole mission of the University, it would be at best entirely useless, if not absolutely injurious to the community in whose midst it might exist.

We know there are many who regard the Common School and the University as being altogether different in their ends, and antagonistic in the influences which they exert over society. But to us they appear as parts of the same great system—both founded on the same principles, and both equally beneficial to the whole mass of the people. To be sure they develop in different degrees the different faculties of human nature; but from this very diversity of action results their unity of purpose. The Common School is more especially engaged in teaching what is considered immediately practical; and in so far as the pure intellect is concerned, looks much more to the cultivation of the perceptive than of the reflective powers. This tendency of the Common School to confine its instruction to those matters more immediately necessary to man in his efforts to get the means of subsistence, is the consequence of the system being instituted for the use of every child in the State, as well as for the reason that those facts which most strongly impress the senses are best adapted for awakening not only the intellect, but also the affections and the moral powers of children. We may say then that the Common School is peculiarly connected with what are generally called the material interests of society. And as man is not single in his nature—inasmuch as he is a mixture of the earthy and celestial—inasmuch as after he has satisfied all his animal wants, he seeks after something loftier and purer—in order to develope all his faculties, the University must be added to and placed above the Common School. In the one the child is taught to read, write and cipher; in the other the youth is led to look more after the true and the beautiful. The University, while it forgets not to inculcate on the scholar the necessity of attending to the material agencies by which we are surrounded, is also occupied with teaching him that there is something more than matter in the universe, and instructs him in the art of removing the integuments which cover over the ideal, and hide from all but the eye-intellectual the beauties and truths of the immaterial world. But since the University is merely a continuation of the Common School, both must be founded on a common principle; both aim, as we have said, at awakening and developing—neither at perfecting—the faculties of our nature.

If we are right in saying that the object of University education is rather to inspire the student with an ardent desire to search after truth, than to infuse into his mind correct opinions on all subjects within the scope of University instruction—it will be immediately perceived that it is much more for the professors and text-writers to be thoroughly imbued with the spirit of a pure and elevated philosophy—than for them to come up to a certain standard of orthodoxy, erected by a certain sect in politics, religion or literature. It was said by Lessing, "If God held in his right hand pure and absolute truth, and in his left only the desire to search after truth, I would tell him to keep pure truth for himself, as mortal eyes are too weak to look on it, and would ask him to give me only the desire to search after truth." So should the youth speak to the professor, if the latter should presume to declare his opinions as the only possible truth, and denounce all others as absolutely and unqualifiedly false. Let the professor rather tell the opinions of others and their reasonings as well as his own; then say to his hearers, "I cannot decide for you, you must inquire and decide for yourselves." Such, we are told, is the course actually pursued by the Lecturer on Constitutional Law in the Law Department of the Louisiana University; and how much better it is than if he merely gave his own opinions, with the reasons which led him to form them, leaving the student under the impression that there was no other rational way of considering the subject!

As with the professors, so should it be with text-books. If we must have text-books on all subjects, entirely free from errors of opinion and doctrine, where shall we find them? not assuredly among the writings of men. Fault has been found with the use of Story and Kent; but where can we find authors who inculcate greater reverence for the constitution, or show themselves more deeply sensible of the patriotic wisdom of the fathers of the Convention? Students, however, will never remain satisfied with a one-sided view of any subject; and having learned from their professors that independence of thought, which is a cardinal virtue in the republic of letters, there is no danger of their receiving the words of any man as the words of a master. Under the judgment of the Professor of Political Economy in our new University, there is no danger of a student imbibing high tariff notions—even if Mr. Peters' Essays on Currency and Commerce should be taken as a text-book.

NOTES

INTRODUCTION: WHITMAN ON THE LEVEE

xvii   **friends with his new landlord:** Whitman's second landlord (at Tremont House) was the wealthy Irish businessman Patrick Irwin (1810–1878). Together with his wife, Irwin was among the select group of friends that attended the funeral of the *Crescent* co-owner Alexander H. Hayes in 1866 ("Funeral of A. H. Hayes, *Times-Picayune*, November 24, 1866). Irwin, like Whitman and other staff members of the *Crescent,* was a Democrat.

xvii   **"in charge":** *Brooklyn Evening Star,* March 15, 1848. Whitman had worked for the *Evening Star* prior to his association with the *Brooklyn Daily Eagle* (1846–48). The latter also reviewed the *Crescent* and discovered Whitman's "handy work in several of its editorials" ("The Crescent," March 14, 1848). The *Atlas,* a sister paper of the *Aurora* that had employed Whitman in 1842, flat-out states that the *Crescent* is solely "edited by Mr. Walter Whitman" ("New Orleans Daily Crescent," May 14, 1848).

xvii   **A painting of . . . Schiller:** "Our talented fellow-citizen, Theodore A. Gould, has left at our office a portrait representing the great German poet, Schiller. . . . it can be seen at our office" ("The Fine Arts," *Daily Crescent,* April 1, 1848).

xviii   **"Really, Gentlemen":** "To our Northern Contemporaries," *Daily Crescent,* March 25, 1848.

xix   **a Klansman:** In 1868, DaPonte gave a twenty-five-minute speech to an assembly of the Seymour Knights before being named an "honorary member" ("The Seymour Knights" *Crescent,* September 16, 1868). The Seymour Knights were a local chapter of the Knights of the White Camellia, which was personally and ideologically interwoven with the Klu Klux Clan. These Knights were a driving force in the Opelousas Massacre, which took place less than two weeks after DaPonte's speech.

xix   **"Jack Waterways":** See "Jack Waterways," *Times-Picayune,* October 7, 1842.

xx   **"Sitting, standing, walking":** "Selections from my Journal, Written During a Sojourn in Louisiana," *Brooklyn Daily Eagle,* February 21, 1851.

xxi   **invited further experimentation:** Sex between men had been legal under French rule but was outlawed in 1805, shortly after the Louisiana Purchase, and since then was punishable by hard labor for life (*Digest of the Penal Law of the State of Louisiana Analytically Arranged* [New Orleans: M. M. Robinson, 1841], 142). There are very few newspaper accounts of the law being enforced, and it is hard to gauge how detrimental its effects were. A report published from 1854 suggests that three men were arrested for the offense in the six months between November 1853 and April 1854; "Office of the Chief of Police," *Times-Picayune,* June 15, 1854.

xxi   **quickly making up stories:** When asked about the "semi-sexual emotions & actions which no doubt do occur between men" by John Addington Symonds in 1890, Whitman not only made the claim of having fathered illegitimate children in New Orleans but replied: "I am fain to hope the pages themselves are not to be even mention'd for such gratuitous and quite at the same time entirely undream'd & unreck'd possibility of morbid inferences—[which] are disavow'd by me & seem damnable" (see *The Correspondence of Walt Whitman: 1890–1892*, vol. 5, ed. Edwin Haviland Miller [New York: New York University Press, 1961], 72–73).

xxii   **newly acquired Mexican territory:** "The question whether or [not] there shall be slavery in the new territories . . . is a question between the *grand body of white workingmen, the millions of mechanics, farmers, and operatives of our country,* with their interests, on the one side— and the interests of the few thousand rich, 'polished', and aristocratic owners of slaves at the south, on the other side" (Whitman, "American Workingmen, versus Slavery," *Brooklyn Daily Eagle,* September 1, 1847).

xxii   **"advocate Free Soil Doctrine":** "Random Recollections," *New Orleans Bulletin,* May 20, 1875.

xxii   **"'T is a rough land":** *The Poetical Works of Fitz-Greene Halleck* (New York: Appleton, 1848), 96–97.

xxiii   **"The principal beauty":** Manhattan, "Northern Correspondence," *Daily Crescent,* September 5, 1848.

xxiv   **"I pride myself":** Quoted in Horace Traubel, *With Walt Whitman in Camden,* vol. 4, ed. Sculley Bradley (Philadelphia: University of Pennsylvania Press, 1953), 49.

xxv   **"Pleased with the native":** *Leaves of Grass* (Brooklyn, 1855, available at the Whitman Archive, www.whitmanarchive.org), 37.

xxv   **Assessment of this sketch:** See, for instance, Jay Grossman, *Reconstituting the American Renaissance: Emerson, Whitman, and the Politics of Representation* (Durham, NC: Duke University Press, 2003), 184; Andrew Lawson, *Walt Whitman & The Class Struggle* (Iowa City: University of Iowa Press, 2006), 41; or Matt Sandler, "Kindred Darkness: Whitman in New Orleans," in *Whitman Noir: Black America and the Good Gray Poet,* ed. Ivy G. Wilson (Iowa City: University of Iowa Press, 2014), 61.

xxvii   **some scholars have even suggested:** For instance, James McWilliams in his "Before a Million Universes," *Paris Review,* May 22, 2017, theparisreview.org/blog/2017/05/22/before-a -million-universes.

PRELUDE: EXCERPTS FROM A TRAVELLER'S NOTE BOOK

Crossing the Alleghanies

1   **interminable brook:** Likely, Whitman is describing the Potomac here.
2   **whilom:** Formerly.

SKETCHES OF NEW ORLEANS

Epigraph

11   *Necessitas non habet* LEG-*em:* A play on the Latin maxim "necessitas non habet legem" (necessity has no law).

Novelties in New Orleans

11   best tooth-brush: Whitman, here and in other pieces, is poking fun at the idea of owning a tooth-brush—a strange, European custom of the rich and cultured at the time. No tooth-brushes were mass produced in the United States in the 1840s, and regular brushing would not become routine until World War II. Whitman's health advice, for example in his *Manly Health and Training* (1858), often borders on the absurd.

11   Santa Anna's favorite passion: One of the favorite past-times of General Antonio López de Santa Anna (1794–1876) was cockfighting. Santa Anna had been defeated by US forces in the US-Mexico War of 1846–48, which had ended just shortly before Whitman set foot on Louisiana soil.

11   Gallic emblem: A rooster, also the emblem of the Democratic Party.

11   "Crow, Chapman—Chapman, crow": The rooster Chapman and this expression are associated in Whitman's time with political victory and the Democratic Party. There are numerous, competing explanations for this saying, one of the oldest harking back to a battle during the war of 1812. As the *St. Louis Democrat* observes in 1885: "At the battle of Lake Champlain there was on board of Commodore McDonough's vessel a crop of poultry. During the engagement, and when the hearts of our brave men were well nigh discouraged . . . a shot from the enemy struck the coop, tearing it to pieces and liberating the inmates. One gallant cock, whom the Bailors bad named Chapman, after one of their messmates, instead of being alarmed at the din around him, flew into the rigging and made the air resound with crow after crow. This incident inspired the men, who responded with hearty cheers and won the day" ("Origin of Popular Phrases," December 21, 1884). An echo of this story can be found in the anecdote of the newspaper editor Chapman, who falsely announced a Democratic victory in the 1840 presidential election with the printing of a rooster: "[P]oor Chapman became the target of his opponents . . . [and] was always known as 'crow, Chapman, crow'" (Frederic Hudson, *Journalism in the United States, from 1690–1872* [New York: Harper & Brothers, 1873], 202).

11   Attakapas bull: A breed favored in bullfighting.

13   "Since Music is the fool of love": From the burlesque opera *Bombastes Furioso* (1810) by English playwright William Barnes Rhodes (1772–1826).

13   to "pink": A gentlemanly poking with a sharp object.

13   Chevalier Bayard: Pierre Terrail, Seigneur de Bayard (ca. 1476–1524), the famous "knight without fear and beyond reproach" also known as "le bon chevalier."

Firemen Celebration

15   "observed of all observers": Shakespeare's Ophelia in *Hamlet,* act 3, scene 1. Much of Whitman's cultural life was shaped by the Bard of Avon: he carried around Shakespeare's poems and later bragged about shouting them from the tops of stagecoaches; many of the bawdy, working-class theater performances he consumed were Shakespeare plays; he memorized long passages from his plays (especially *Richard II*); later in life, he even participated in the debates around Shakespearean authorship. Nonetheless, Whitman ultimately judged Shakespeare too "feudal" in his political outlook.

15   George W. Harby, Esq.: George Washington Harby (1797–1862), a local teacher and fireman.

15   Messrs. Clark & Hickok: The New Commercial Exchange was located on the corner of St. Charles and Perdido streets. Mr. Hickok is likely Captain Daniel Starr Hickok (1811–1880), a showman, regatta organizer, and famous hotelier. His co-owner, Clark, was also described as a "captain" ("Juleps!" *Daily Delta,* May 7, 1847).

15   "red wine freely flowed": Exact source unclear.

15   "Blessed the beeves": Source of quote is unclear. Perhaps Whitman is misconstruing a Homer quote from memory, most likely a passage from Book XV, which mentions the consumption of "a-good-feast of flesh, and dulcet wine" (Lovelace Bigge-Wither, *A Nearly Literal Translation of Homer's Odyssey Into Accentuated Dramatic Verse* [James Paker and Co: Oxford, UK, 1869], 269). "Beeves" and "kine" are both archaic terms for cattle, with a strong culinary association. Alongside "dulcet wine," they occur frequently in Alexander Pope's translations of the *Iliad* and the *Odyssey,* though never, it appears, in a similar couplet.

The Sabbath

15   silver Tweed nor the green-fringed Clyde: A reference to Wordsworth's 1803 poem "Yarrow Unvisited." Whitman had an intense interest in the British Romantics in the late 1840s and early 1850s, though his assessment varied from enthusiastic to skeptical. In 1849, in the margins of a magazine piece on the Romantics, Whitman announced: "Wordsworth lacks sympathy with men and women" ("Christopher under Canvass [marginalia]," available at the Whitman Archive).

16   argossie: A merchant ship.

16   "a loving community": Exact source unclear. The King James Bible does not use the term "community." The *Book of Common Prayer* (first published in 1549), invoked by Whitman elsewhere in this volume, uses similar terms to describe the Trinity.

Daguerreotype Portraits

16   Shade of Daguerre: Daguerreotyping, named after its inventor, Louis Daguerre (1787–1851), was the first widely available photographic process. Whitman's image in the front of this volume is the oldest extant daguerreotype of the poet and was likely taken in New Orleans. Whitman's marvel at the mundane yet magical process of arresting one's image on a metal plate may have inspired this humorous sketch. Daguerreotypes did not capture color.

17   Phœbus: Greek God of light.

18   "can such things be": *Macbeth,* act 3, scene 4.

"The Season," Hereabouts

18   Our Northern friends: Whitman's "Northern friends"—in the form of his old employer, the *Brooklyn Daily Eagle*—took note and reprinted parts of this piece ("The season in N. Orleans," March 18, 1848).

Mardi Gras

19   "turbaned Moor": *Othello,* act 5, scene 2.

20   "Paddy gave the drum": A beating. "Paddy" was a commonly used slang term for the Irish. See also Joann P. Krieg's *Whitman and the Irish* (Iowa City: University of Iowa Press, 2000), available at the Whitman Archive.

20   "snack it": The poet Byron died fighting the Ottomans for Greek independence in 1824, nine years before King Otto became the first monarch of an independent Greece. He would have been around seventeen at the time of Byron's death. Perhaps Whitman is misremembering facts here. While Byron suffered from anorexia nervosa and the culinary association of "snack" did exist, the *Webster's Dictionary* of 1846 also defines it as "a share."

21   "penny-a-liner": A derogatory term for a newspaper scribbler; one who gets paid "by the line."

21   "Take to something of more serious method": A reference to *Richard III,* act 1, scene 2: "To leave the keen encounter of your tongues / And fall to something of more serious method."

The Habitants of Hotels

22   cock-pit: Cockfighting ring.

22   "Count D'Orsay": Famous French dandy and painter Alfred d'Orsay (1801–1852). See illustration on page 38.

22   pallid proboscis: his long nose. Literally: long appendage on an animal's face (for instance, an elephant's trunk).

22   Emanuel Swedenborg: The Christian mystic Swedenborg (1688–1772) had a profound influence on American literature through Emerson and the Transcendentalists. Whitman's (positive) take on Swedenborg can be found in his "Who Was Swedenborg?" (*Brooklyn Daily Times,* May 15, 1858).

22   Mesmerism: A pseudoscience centered on a quasi-electric life force often termed "animal magnetism," proposed by the German doctor Franz Mesmer (1734–1815). Mesmer's theories seem to have influenced some of Whitman's writings, including perhaps his "I Sing the Body Electric."

22   chloroform: The *Crescent* in these years filled many an editorial page with debates on the dangers and benefits of chloroform. See for instance "Caution, but not Prohibition," of March 6, 1848.

22   "Model Artists": A troupe that performed *tableaux vivants* in the nude—that is, they posed naked to mirror ancient statues. Not surprisingly, the audience was overwhelmingly male. See Appendix B.

22   "lion of the day": A celebrated person or object of intense interest.

23   Kirby: J. Hudson Kirby (1810–1848), a London-born actor and "idol of the cheap theatres of his day" (Gerald Martin Bordman, *The Concise Oxford Companion to American Theatre* [Oxford, UK: Oxford University Press, 1987], 253).

23   "b'hoys": B'hoys (and the female "b'ghals") were working-class street toughs, often associated with the Bowery in New York, but springing up in all major cities of the United States in the late 1840s. The slang term itself mimics Irish pronunciation of "boy" and "girl."

23   N. P. Willis: Nathaniel Parker Willis (1806–1867), a famous editor and one of the best-paid magazine writers of his day, especially known for his travel writings. Whitman had worked with him at the *New York Mirror* shortly before coming to New Orleans.

23   Mike Walsh: Michael Walsh (1810–1859) was an editor, a major Democratic player, a nativist, and the leader of the violent "Spartan Band" faction of antiestablishment Democrats. Whitman had written for Walsh's paper early in his career and considered him and the Spartans to be of "true Blue American spirit."

23   "hoss": A strong (working-class) man; a manly man; the real deal.

23   "the Brigadier": Perhaps a reference to Brigadier General Robert Swartwout (1779–1848), who was serving on the Board of Aldermen for New York's Third Ward at the time of publication of this piece. Swartwout had achieved fame during the War of 1812, became an establishment Democrat, and also served New York's Fifth Ward as alderman.

23   "A hickory stick and a hickory soul": Here Whitman might be invoking "Old Hickory"— Andrew Jackson (1767–1845)—to suggest a workman's toughness.

23   "Union" and "National Intelligencer": The *Daily Union* and the *National Intelligencer* were daily newspapers from Washington, DC, the former leaning Democratic and the latter Whig.

23   Robert Peel and John Russell . . . Louis Philippe . . . Prince Metternich: Whitman is listing leading European politicians here: Robert Peel (1788–1850) and John Russell (1792–1878) were British prime ministers, the former Conservative, the latter Liberal. Louis Philippe I (1773–1850), the last king of France (in power 1830–48). Klemens von Metternich (1773–1859) was an Austrian diplomat who played a key role in reshaping Europe after the end of the Napoleonic Wars (Congress of Vienna, 1814–15) and was subsequently toppled by the liberal revolutions of 1848.

Sketches of the Sidewalks and Levee: Peter Funk, Esq.

24   Peter Funk: a term commonly used to describe mock bidders. It likely originated in Asa Green's New York tale *The Perils of Pearl Street, Including A Taste of the Dangers of Wall Street* (New York: Betts & Anstice, and Peter Hill, 1834). Peter Funks were considered a real problem at the day—the *Crescent* during Whitman's tenure would, for instance, comment on legislation being passed to curtail this nuisance.

24   "life, fortune and sacred honor": Last line of the US Declaration of Independence.

25   "the last rose of summer": Title of an 1805 poem by Irish poet Thomas Moore (1779–1852). Whitman was invited to the Moore centenary in New York but did not go, likely due to ill health. Even later in life, Whitman listed Moore alongside Scott and Burns as one of the few "very consoling" authors he would revisit "again and again in certain humors" (in Horace Traubel, *With Walt Whitman in Camden*, vol. 2 [New York: Mitchell Kennerly, 1915], 55).

25   *non est inventus*: Legal response by a sheriff when a defendant cannot be located. Literally: "he or she has not been found."

26   *rotundo:* Literally "round," used to refer to a round building. Perhaps Whitman is imagining a military sense of the word here (like "a round of shots").

27   *argal:* therefore.

28   "The native hue": *Hamlet,* act 3, scene 1.

28   "for the morrow": likely from Matthew 6:34. "Take therefore no thought for the morrow: for the morrow shall take thought for the things of itself. Sufficient unto the day is the evil thereof."

Sketches of the Sidewalks and Levee: Miss Dusky Grisette

28   Mademoiselle Grisette: A "grisette" is working woman, a term that by the nineteenth century had come to suggest prostitution.

28   "buy a broom" style: Likely a reference to Edward Knight's 1827 "Buy a Broom" ditty that features a girl singing in heavy dialect—in this case: German, but mirroring minstrel intonation—selling her wares and warning of infidelity: "Buy a broom, buy a Broom, pretty Boom, I sing. Pretty little Broom is of much use when your lover go astray. Should de fond one ever you abuse, you den whip him away wid de Broom" (Edward Knight, *Buy a Broom? Mrs. Knight's Celebrated Song of Buy a Broom: Sung by Her with the Most Enthusiastic Applause* [Philadelphia: G. Willig, 1827]).

28   *em bon point:* Used to refer to women's "ample part" or bosom.

28   "silence that speaks": Slightly incorrect (wrong tense) rendition of Homer's *Iliad* (Book XIV) in Pope's translation.

29   "but that's not much": *Othello,* act 3, scene 3; a reference to infidelity.

29   "Night / Shows stars": From Lord Byron's *Don Juan* (1819–24). Byron (1788–1824) could well be called a "gay icon" of his day, though the terminology would, of course, be anachronistic: the originally medical definition of homosexuality as well as the modern concept of sexual orientation did not exist at the time. Whitman could quote the British Romantic from memory by the 1840s and even late in life observed to a friend that "Byron has fire enough to burn forever."

30   "all things to all men": 1 Corinthians 9:19–23, in which Apostle Paul speaks: "I am made all things to all men, that I might by all means save some" (King James Bible).

Celebration of St. Patrick's Day

31   Hibernian Society: The Ancient Order of Hibernians is an Irish-Catholic fraternal society, advocating for the Irish in the United States as well as for Irish independence abroad. The *Crescent* staff had members associated with the group.

Hebrew Benevolent Association Ball

32   St. Louis: The St. Louis Hotel, on the corner of St. Louis and Chartres streets, remembered fondly by Whitman for its "particularly grand" barrooms. See his "New Orleans in 1848," in this volume.

32   **death and disease:** In 1847, New Orleans suffered from a major outbreak of yellow fever, which was covered by a number of northern newspapers, including the *Brooklyn Daily Eagle,* which called the disease "The Scourge of the South" (September 14, 1847). Due to its frequent disease outbreaks, the Crescent City was also nicknamed "Necropolis of the South" (Jo Ann Carrigan, *The Saffron Scourge: A History of Yellow Fever in Louisiana, 1796–1905* [Lafayette: University of Louisiana at Lafayette Press, 2015], 48–49).

32   **Arabian Nights:** The folktale collection *Arabian Nights* was Whitman's self-described first formative reading experience (*Complete Prose Works* [Philadelphia: David McKay, 1892], 15). He would frequently reference it in his writings, for instance telling a friend in old age: "if I had the magic carpet of the Arabian Nights, I should come down & join your circle for a couple of hours" ("Walt Whitman to Susan Stafford, 14 May 1882," Whitman Archive).

32   **"mortals of clay":** 2 Corinthians 4:7. "And the LORD God formed man of the dust of the ground, and breathed into his nostrils the breath of life; and man became a living soul" (King James Bible).

32   **The loveliness of the fair "Daughters of Israel":** Whitman echoed this orientalization of Jewish women in a number of his writings, for instance when informing his readers that he lost track of the proceedings at a New York synagogue upon being confronted with the sight of beautiful "dark-eyed Jewesses" seated across from him ("Doings at the Synagogue," *New York Aurora,* March 29, 1842). Whitman's novel *Jack Engle* also includes an underdeveloped side plot about a Jewish woman and her "showy looking black-eyed daughter Rebecca," who is a "good specimen of Israelitish beauty" (*Life and Adventures of Jack Engle: An Auto-Biography,* ed. Zachary Turpin [Iowa City: University of Iowa Press, 2017], 71, 22).

33   **Naiades from the sea:** Naiads are river spirits in ancient Greek mythology, often depicted as female.

Health and Cleanliness

33   **a powerful influence on the summer health:** Whitman, like many of his contemporaries, believed that street hygiene had a direct effect on diseases like cholera.

Sketches of the Sidewalks and Levee: Daggerdraw Bowieknife, Esq.

34   **"I take my pen in hand":** A common phrase to open a letter—so common, indeed that it was taught as part of composition and rote memorization exercises in American schools at the time (Warren Burton, *The District School, as It Was. By One Who Went to It* [Boston: Philips, Sampson & Co., 1850], 181). The sixth section of Whitman's autobiographical "Calamus Leaves" (included in this volume) begins with the question "What think you I have taken my pen to record?" later changed by Whitman to "What think you I take my pen in hand to record?"

34   **"Freeze my young blood":** *Hamlet,* act 1, scene 5.

35   **"pass by as the idle wind":** *Julius Caesar,* act 4, scene 3.

35   **"disciple of Blackstone":** William Blackstone (1723–80) wrote one the foundational works

of British common law, *Commentaries on the Laws of England* (1765–70), which also proved highly influential on the development of the legal system of the United States.

36 "There was a lurking devil": From Byron's *Corsair* (1814). See also page 137.

36 "And the Lord set a mark upon Cain": Genesis 4:15. Whitman is quoting the King James Bible.

36 Bob Acres: A character from Richard Brinsley Sheridan's comic play *The Rivals* (1775), and his speech in act 4, scene 1. Whitman adored Sheridan (1751–1816) and in editorials for New York papers would invoke the Irish playwright in the same breath as Cicero. The original line reads "This is my return for getting him before all his brothers and sisters!" Whitman, who will reference the same play in his "Letters from a Travelling Bachelor" a year later, appears to have memorized passages from it.

36 "tired nature's sweet restorer": From John Mitford Edward Young's "Nine Thoughts" (1834), often misattributed to Shakespeare.

36 Banquo: A loyal ally, murdered by Macbeth after a prophecy suggests that Banquo's lineage will outlive Macbeth's.

Sketches of the Sidewalks and Levee: John J. Jinglebrain

37 "The lines are fallen": Psalm 16:6, originally spoken in first person. The second part of the sentence—"yea, I have a goodly heritage"—is noticeably absent.

37 "the ton": A French term, meaning "style."

38 Shakspeare: A valid, preferred spelling at the time.

38 "the tailor made him": *King Lear,* act 2, scene 2.

38 Man is an eating animal: Variations of this phrase are used throughout the nineteenth century in philosophical and scientific discourse, generally as an homage to Erasmus Darwin, who is believed to have originated it ("Man is an eating animal, a drinking animal, and a sleeping animal, and one placed in a material world"). It was invoked widely, including by the phrenologist Orson Squire Fowler, who would analyze Whitman's skull shape in the summer of 1848.

39 Fanny Kemble: A famous British actress (1809–1893), much admired by Whitman. Whitman also praises her in a letter to the *Crescent* of August 14, 1848.

The Nights of New Orleans

40 "glides like a silver shield": Unidentified.

41 "lovely skies of Italy": Unidentified. The phrase occurs in an 1839 poem by poet and future Confederate privateer John Newland Maffitt (1819–1886), but that is unlikely to be the source.

In the Wrong Box

41 "waved her nimble feet": Perhaps a reference to Lord Byron's "The Waltz" (1813), though it does not contain the line verbatim. Instead we find: "Her nimble feet danced off another's head; / Not Cleopatra on her galley's deck." See also page 137.

Serious but Ludicrous Accident

42   "from the sublime to the ridiculous": Famous quote often attributed to French author Bernard Le Bouyer de Fontenelle (1657–1757).

43   John Minor Botts: Virginia representative (1802–1869), who famously pledged to "head" President Tyler (1790–1862)—that is, impeach him—"or die." He did neither.

43   "were ish mine horse and cart": Whitman, himself of Dutch stock, was partial to stereotypical depictions of brash, business-minded "Dutchmen." He, for instance, read the following words in an 1846 article and annotated them as "True words about the Dutch": "We can hardly hear or speak or think of a Dutchman without calling up to mental vision a short, stumpy, obese personage, with heavy face, bullet head, rolling gait, arrayed in vestments ample alike in number and dimensions, marvelously sparing of words, but prodigal of tobacco-smoke" ("Longfellow's Poets and Poetry of Europe [marginalia]," Whitman Archive). Whitman, ever fond of dialects, late in life disclosed that one of his "favorite stories" is that "of the Dutchman—a miller—who would say, 'Vell, vat do I care for vere die veat comes from, so it is good?'" (in Horace Traubel, With Walt Whitman in Camden, vol. 5, ed. Gertrude Traubel [Carbondale: Southern Illinois University Press, 1964], 451.).

New Orleans in Mud

43   "day that tried the soles": The phrase "The day that tried the souls of men" was often used to describe the day the United States declared independence.

Razors, Reason, and Resolution

44   poetry in turnips: Walter Scott (1771–1832) had commented in a letter: "Poetry is a scourging crop, and ought not to be hastily repeated. Editing, therefore, may be considered as a green crop of turnips or peas, extremely useful to those whose circumstances do not admit of giving their farm a summer fallow" (in William Hickling Prescott, Biographical and Critical Miscellanies [New York: Harper & Brothers, 1845], 172). Whitman fell in love with Scott's works as a young child, and they remained a "chief pleasure" into old age (in Horace Traubel, With Walt Whitman in Camden, vol. 2 [New York: Mitchell Kennerly, 1915], 251).

44   "Razor Strop Man": Henry Smith (1815–1889), the self-proclaimed "original Razor Strop Man," was a bit of a cult figure with the Washingtonians, a working-class temperance movement that Whitman supported in his early years, prompting him to write the popular anti-alcohol novel Franklin Evans, or: The Inebriate (1842). Songs, poems, and even an autobiography of sorts by "The Celebrated Razor Strop Man" might have been familiar to Whitman in these years. The Brooklyn Daily Eagle, under Whitman's editorship, even updated their readership about the whereabouts of the man ("The Razor Strop Man . . . sojourns in the interior of Virginia, somewhere," it noted in June of 1846). A sarcastic 1860 review of Leaves of Grass even noted that one could perceive "the eloquence of the Razor-Strop man" in Whitman's verse (Southern Field and Fireside, June 9, 1860).

46   "some, and no mistake": A common saying at the time, meaning "a force to be reckoned with" or "of importance."

Visit of a Distinguished Personage

46   Mr. Henry Smith: See page 140.

46   the Sun office: In 1842, Whitman had published a story in the *Sun*, an at times sensational publication aimed at the literate working class. Its office was located in Newspaper Row, a neighborhood quite familiar to Whitman.

Non-Ascension of the Balloon

47   "finding that turf was": Variant of the common expression "finding *X* of no avail, had recourse to *Y*," exact source unclear.

Who Shall Wear Motley?

48   Motley: A jester's costume.

Day after the Election!

49   Day after the Election: The municipal elections of April 3, 1848, resulted in a continuation of the Whig status quo. As the *Crescent* put it: "The Day was fine, and the election was conducted with the decorum which characterizes such an occasion in New Orleans. There was very little interest taken in the contest by the great body of the citizens" ("The Election," *Daily Crescent*, April 4, 1848). This sketch echoes a critique of politicians (of either party) motivated by self-interest that we find again in Whitman's later novella *Jack Engle,* parts of which he was likely composing in the 1840s.

49   "a white stone": Revelation 2:17. "He that hath an ear, let him hear what the Spirit saith unto the churches; To him that overcometh will I give to eat of the hidden manna, and will give him a white stone, and in the stone a new name written, which no man knoweth saving he that receiveth *it*" (King James Bible).

49   "never say fail": Taken from the 1839 play *Richelieu; Or the Conspiracy* by Edward Bulwer-Lytton (1803–1873) about the seventeenth-century French statesman Cardinal Richelieu (1803–1873). *Richelieu* also originated the famous saying "The pen is mightier than the sword."

Strangers, Beware!

51   Pickpockets: Whitman, who certainly stood out in crowd, was an easy target for pickpockets. After losing all his money to the "profession" *en route* to Washington, DC, in the 1860s, one of his publishers "could not repress the facetious comment that any pickpocket who failed to avail himself of such an opportunity as Walt offered, with loose baggy trousers, and no suspenders, would have been a disgrace to his profession," as Ellen M. Calder recalled in 1907 (*Atlantic Monthly* 99, 826). Whitman, by then, was fond of wearing women's pants, called "bloomers."

51   **as Jack Falstaff says:** The humorous character John Falstaff appears in Shakespeare's *Henry IV, Henry V,* and *The Merry Wives of Windsor.* The exact quote does not appear to exist.

The Balloon Blow Up

51   **mysterious French name:** The *Crescent* variously referred to her as Madame "Renards" and "Bernard." Other papers called her "Renard."

Lafayette Square

53   **"same old square":** Perhaps Whitman is thinking of "To this same place, to this same monument," uttered by Balthasar, not Mercutio, at the conclusion of *Romeo and Juliet.*
53   **"anan, anan!":** *Henry IV,* Part 1, act 2, scene 4.

Vagrants

54   **"Can the beauty of the rose":** Origin unclear.
54   **steps . . . seen by Jacob:** Jacob's Ladder, in Genesis 28:10–17.

The Old Cathedral

54   **The Old Cathedral:** St. Louis Cathedral, then known as the Cathedral Chartres & Orleans, situated between the Courthouse and the Old Prison. Whitman is describing the structure before it was remodeled in 1850.

The "News Boys." A Street Conversation

56   **a confab:** Whitman, like many of his contemporaries, enjoyed street urchin tales. In *Jack Engle,* he also depicts a physical altercation between two young "Masters" of the streets in a similarly humorous fashion. Perhaps Whitman, oversized and graying before his time, is self-inserting here, and we can hear him utter the kind words of the "elderly gentleman, tall and masculine." Whitman's 1842 writings for the *Aurora* contain similar sketches.
57   **House of Reffurage:** A House of Refuge was opened in New Orleans in 1845 to rehabilitate juvenile offenders.

Sketches of the Sidewalks and Levee: Timothy Goujon, V.O.N.O.

59   **V.O.N.O.:** Likely a playful riff on fraternal societies, which were widely popular in New Orleans, as in the rest of the country. A number of senior staff members at the *Crescent* were members of the benevolent Independent Order of Odd Fellows and would indicate their membership by adding abbreviations like "I.O.O.F." to their names.
59   **ycleped:** meaning "called," archaic.
59   **oysters:** Whitman enjoyed oysters so much, he would eat them for breakfast. In a later,

anonymous self-review for the *Brooklyn Daily Times,* he describes himself as someone who "likes a supper of oysters fresh from the oyster-smack—likes to make one at the crowded table among sailors and workpeople—would leave a select soiree of elegant people any time to go with tumultuous men" (review at Whitman Archive).

59   *ecaillé:* translates to "shell."

60   "who runs may read": Habakkuk 2:2.

60   "the dome of thought": From Lord Byron's *Childe Harold's Pilgrimage* (1812–18). See also page 137.

60   "Pharaoh's lean kine": *Henry IV, Part 1,* act 2.

61   "is the gift of nature": *Much Ado about Nothing,* act 1, scene 2.

61   *sans culottes:* translates to "without breeches." It was a term to the lower classes during the French *Ancien Régime* and a symbol of the impoverished revolutionary.

61   "most senseless and fit": *Much Ado about Nothing,* act 3, scene 3.

61   "this breathing world": *Richard III,* act 1, scene 1.

61   "featherless bipeds": Plato's (ca. 425–ca. 348 BC) humorous description of a human. Whitman evokes Plato directly and indirectly in a number of his later poems (such as his 1871 "The Base of All Metaphysics").

62   *viva voce:* translates to "by word of mouth," "orally." Literally: With living voice.

62   *sang froid:* translates to "with composure."

62   "most congregate": *The Merchant of Venice,* act 1 scene 3.

62   "veni ici tout de suite": roughly translates to "Come! Right here, right now."

62   "poisson de la mer": translates to "fish of the sea."

62   "bonne huîtres": translates to "good oysters."

62   *chuqu' un a son goût,* and *chaqu' un a son gré:* should be: "à chacun son goût ("to each his own taste") and "chacun a son gré" (roughly: "each in his own way").

Sketches of the Sidewalks and Levee: Mrs. Giddy Gay Butterfly

62   "blessed womenkind": "blessed womankind" does appear in letter by Scott.

63   "sealed with seven seals": Revelation 5:1.

63   "chill November's surly blast": From "Man Was Made to Mourn: A Dirge" (1784) by Scottish poet Robert Burns (1759–1796). In his 1886 essay "Robert Burns as Poet and Person," Whitman claims that "[n]ever indeed was there truer utterance in a certain range of idiosyncracy than by this poet," and "no man that ever lived . . . was so fondly loved, both by men and women, as Robert Burns" (*Complete Prose Works* [Philadelphia: David McKay, 1891], 399).

64   "declined into the vale": *Othello,* act 3, scene 3.

64   meed: a deserved share.

64   Martineau: Harriet Martineau (1802–1876) was an English author and social theorist.

64   "silks and satins fine": A common literary phrase, often used in association with pirates.

64   "golden calves": Reference to Exodus 32.

64   "besetting sin": A common expression at the time, likely originating in Hebrews 12:1, which calls on believers to "let us lay aside every weight, and the sin which doth so easily beset us, and let us run with patience the race that is set before us" (King James Bible).

65   "sowing with the wind": Hosea 8:7. "For they have sown the wind, and they shall reap the whirlwind."

65   "Just as the twig": Common proverb in eighteenth-century England. Here from Alexander Pope's 1732 *Moral Essays* (also known as *Epistles to Several Persons*).

65   *res augustæ domi:* "Res angusta domi" literally translates to "poor circumstances at home" and is especially used to refer to the pressures of poverty, a connotation likely lost on Whitman.

66   "silk purse . . . pig's ear": A common proverb, akin to "turning lemons into lemonade" (that is, something unpleasant into a thing of value).

66   "way that he should go": Proverbs 22:6. "Train up a child in the way he should go: and when he is old, he will not depart from it" (King James Bible).

Sketches of the Sidewalks and Levee: Patrick McDray

66   Hibernian: an Irishman. See also page 137.

66   that's a Patrick McDray: Whitman paints a stereotyped but overall positive picture of a "Paddy" here that avoids some of the vitriol (excessive drinking coupled with violence, anti-republican treachery, electioneering, Papism, and so forth) often present in depictions of the Irish at the time. A "drayman" is a laborer who delivers beer.

66   "ghost from the grave": Perhaps a *Hamlet* reference.

66   "There's nought but care": from "Green Grow the Rashes, O" (1783) by Robert Burns. Coupled with the last name McDray, it might suggest Scots-Irish lineage. See also page 143.

67   "virtue, liberty and independence": Revolutionary motto, later adopted as the state motto of Pennsylvania.

67   "uses of adversity": Shakespeare's *As You Like It,* act 2, scene 1. Here it alludes to the Great Famine of 1845, which drove much of the Irish immigration to the United States. The famine, which killed millions, was most proximately triggered by potato blight, but its root causes lay with English policy towards Ireland: absentee landlordism coupled with tenant farming, infrastructural neglect, and an overreliance on potato monoculture. Whitman, later in life, became a sympathizer toward Irish-nationalist causes.

68   "O Nature! all thy shows": from "To William Simpson of Ochiltree" by Robert Burns (1785). See also page 143.

68   "world of care": from Lord Byron's "Ode (from the French)." See also page 137.

68   "rale Tipperary": She behaves like a full-blooded Irish woman. Tipperary is a region in south-central Ireland.

68   Cashel: Term for an Irish fortress.

68   "darkened counsel": Job 38:2. "Who *is* this that darkeneth counsel by words without knowledge?"

A Walk about Town: By a Pedestrian

69   wished I owned the negro: A starling statement, even as a hypothetical. Whitman had a soft spot for horses and was apparently appalled by some of the cruelty to animals he witnessed in New Orleans. "Is there no Municipal ordinance existing relative to maimed horses?" the

Crescent (perhaps Whitman) inquired of its readers in early May: "Yesterday, towards eve-ning, on walking down Magazine street, we saw a noble looking horse . . . standing on three legs, the fourth hanging in the most cruelly mutilated condition from his body. . . . There he stood, suffering all that man could possibly suffer with a broken leg, while the owner was doubtless cursing only the chance that injured his pocket" ("Inhumanity to Animals," May 6, 1848).

69   long-shoreman: A dockworker.

69   tippler's shop: A tippler is a habitual drinker.

69   bastinadoed: A caning or whipping of the feet, often used as corporal punishment in schools (a practice Whitman vehemently opposed).

69   stevedores: Workers who stow cargo on board of ships (as opposed to longshoremen, who work the docks).

69   "tired nature's sweet restorer": See page 139.

70   St. Mary's Market: Then located at the junction of Annunciation and Tchoupitoulas streets but ordered removed by the city in 1858.

70   a disciple of Graham: Grahamites were a favorite punchline in Whitman's editorials in these days. Sylvester Graham (1794–1851) was a social and dietary reformer, well-known for his vegetarianism and defense of bland foods, which he believed to be a useful anti-masturbation aid. Graham crackers, developed for this purpose, were named after him.

70   cute: here, meaning "clever."

To the Seekers of Pleasure

71   b'hoys: See page 136.

71   "most do congregate": *The Merchant of Venice*, act 1, scene 3.

71   "Washington Hotel. Messrs. Kennedy & Co.": There are a number of "puffs" like these in the *Crescent*, for which Whitman was very likely responsible. These include praises of his friend Thomas Gould, a local painter, ice-cream parlors (run by New Yorkers), oyster bars—and Carrollton hotels. Whitman, a former schoolteacher, may have first come to Carrollton to witness teaching demonstrations at local schools (covered by the *Crescent*). Puffs were stan-dard practice for Whitman (for example at the *Aurora* or the *Brooklyn Daily Eagle*).

Steam Stronger Than Shot

72   hoss: See page 136.

72   "Them Mexicans": The victorious US-Mexico War had just come to an end. Initially Whit-man supported the war effort and favored large-scale acquisition of Mexican lands as an ex-tension of republicanism—an attitude he later came to regret. In his prose recollections ti-tled *Specimen Days*, he named Mexico the "only [country] to whom we have ever really done wrong" ([Philadelphia: Rees Welsh & Co, 1882], 64). Fierce disagreement over the extension of slavery into the newly acquired territories (especially in the form of the 1846 Wilmot Pro-viso) was one of the foundational moments of the democratic schism between Free Soilers and establishment Hunkers.

72   "potater rot": A reference to the potato famine in Ireland. Meaning: this person is Irish. See
      also page 144.

72   John Donkeys: castrated mules.

72   breasted balls: A testicular term since the fourteenth century—and, coupled with the "John
      Donkey" just a few words previous, perhaps a bit of intended wordplay.

A Sabbath Sketch: Or, Going to and Coming from Church

73   "all that in them were": Source unclear. Perhaps it is taken from the anonymously published
      1793 *The Genius of Shakspear, a Summer Dream* (London: Couch and Laking), where the line
      references the inhabitants of the afterlife.

73   Leghorn hats: straw hats.

Public Squares

75   Queen Mab: Folkloric fairy, here likely via Mercutio's speech in Shakespeare's *Romeo and
      Juliet*.

75   "light fantastic toe": From John Milton's pastoral poem "L'Allegro" (1645). Whitman quotes
      from the same poem in his 1858 *Manly Health and Training*.

A Night at the Terpsichore Ball: By "You Know Who"

76   Terpsichore Ball: Terpsichore Hall stood in what is today the Garden District of New Or-
      leans and what was then the independent city of Lafayette (incorporated in 1852). The ball-
      room was located on Rosseau Street on the block between Soraparu and Philip streets. It
      burned down in 1850.

76   Old Bachelor Society: Bachelordom, at times a euphemism for queer sexual expression, was
      actually discussed as a problem in New Orleans, then overflowing with single men (soldiers,
      traders, and so forth). Local papers even proposed significantly increasing the tax burden on
      single men (incrementally by age) to entice them to become productive members of society
      and not squander their income just on themselves ("Taxing Bachelors," *Times-Picayune*, Feb-
      ruary 16, 1840).

77   Japhet: One of the three sons of Noah, who discovered his drunken father "uncovered
      within his tent" (Genesis 9:21, King James Bible).

77   Lafayette car: Horse-drawn cars left from the Railroad Depot on St. Charles Street, turning
      onto Jackson Avenue toward the Mississippi.

77   "Old Dan Tucker": Famous American folk song, at times performed in blackface, dealing
      with the exploits of its eponymous character upon his arrival in a strange town.

77   postoffice on advertising days: Prior to the widespread use of stamps and standardized re-
      ceiving addresses, letters would generally be stored at a local post office and picked up (and
      paid for) by their recipients. Whitman is referring to the day lists of recipients were adver-
      tised, for instance, in newspapers, indicating they had letters to pick up—and resulting in a
      massive rush to the post office.

78   cotillion: A popular group dance.

78   Doctor Collyer: Robert Hanham Collyer (1814–1891) was the owner of the Model Artists troupe; see page 135. He also had an interest in the occult and pseudosciences like mesmerism. In 1845, Collyer wrote to Edgar Allan Poe about his story "The Facts in the Case of M. Valdemar," exclaiming: "I have not the least doubt of the *possibility* of such a phenomenon; for I did actually restore to active animation a person who died from excessive drinking of ardent spirits" (in *Edgar Allan Poe: His Life, Letters, and Opinions,* ed. John H. Ingram [London: W. H. Allen, 1886], 277).

78   Dryden down to James: John Dryden (1631–1700), likely know to Whitman through the work of Dryden's editor, Walter Scott. The reference to "James" is unclear—perhaps it is Henry James Pye (1744–1813).

79   speak openly: Such transgression was encouraged during events like these. As Whitman's acquaintance Thomas Gould would reminisce years later about a similar event: "Oh, dear! what joy it was to thus be at liberty to question the pretty dears! It is only the maskers who are privileged to address ladies who are stranger to them. A lady in mask who would freely take the arm of a mask that might be a stranger to her, never would think of taking so great a liberty did she not deem herself perfectly safe from recognition" ("Sections from my Journal, written during a Sojourn in Louisiana," *Brooklyn Daily Eagle,* February 27, 1851). Apparently, the balls at Terpsichore were known for such behavior. In an ad for a masked ball in late 1848 the proprietor pledged "his best exertions to make the Terpsichore a respectable and agreeable resort, and to maintain the strictest order and decorum" ("Terpsichore Hall, Lafayette," *Times-Picayune,* November 29, 1848).

79   Morpheus: Greek god of sleep.

Sketches of the Sidewalks and Levee: Doctor Sangrado Snipes

79   Sangrado: an archaic term for a quack.

79   "breathing world": *Richard III,* act 1, scene 1.

80   "Scarce half made up": *Richard III,* act 1, scene 1.

80   like Samson's *foxes:* reference to Judges 15:4, which tells the story of military leader Samson, setting hundreds of foxes ablaze, letting them torch the crops of the Philistines.

80   phylacterics: ancient scrolls.

80   "duly armed and equipped": Common legal expression.

80   *secundum artem:* Following accepted practice.

80   "death on fits": "fits" are seizures. Snipes is a "killer doctor" for seizures.

80   "bread-eating, clothes-wearing animal": See page 139.

80   "wherewith to eat": Matthew 6:31. "What shall we eat? or, What shall we drink? or, Wherewithal shall we be clothed?" (King James Bible).

81   Baron Wenzel: Michael de Wenzel (1724–1790) was the eye doctor (oculist) of King George III. His specialty was cataract treatment. For his precision and speed—thirty seconds per cataract surgery—he became known as "Wenzel the knife."

81   "that I must have spoiled": The source for this quote cannot be located, but the *Transactions of the Medical Association of Georgia* of 1892 includes a performative thanks to Asclepius, God

of Medicine, for providing his daughter Hygeia with the "nerve to destroy a hat full of good eyes to learn how to successfully remove the crystalline lenses from a defective eye"—the procedure Wenzel was known for. Whether Wenzel actually uttered the words or not, they were associated with him and represent the attitude of the medical profession at the time. Medical education in the first half of the nineteenth century was split into a lecture-based, entirely theoretical college education (a relative novelty at the time), followed by a rather informal apprenticeship with an established doctor. Actual training—as Whitman observes—was performed largely on live patients.

81   "I've tried it on a dog": From John Tobin's (1770–1804) comedy *The Honeymoon* (1805), act 4, scene 2. The quote refers to bloodletting.

81   Galenic art: Galen of Pergamon (ca. 129–216) was one of the most influential medical experts of Western antiquity.

82   old Boniface's ale: Saint Boniface was the Catholic converter of many German pagans to Christianity and patron saint of Germany, tailors—and brewers. Whether Boniface, who, among other things, persuaded heathens to stop sacrificing beer to their gods, did so primarily out of a love of ale is questionable.

82   *Gil Blas:* a widely influential rags-to-riches novel by Alain-René Lesage (1668–1747) that follows a working-class man as he succeeds in a corrupt society by relying not on his upbringing but his wits. It was published in several parts between 1715 and 1735.

82   *ars diabolocus:* Devil's technique, wicked arts.

82   ipecacuanha: A vomit-inducing drug (now known as "ipecac"), derived from the South American plant of the same name, then used largely to treat dysentery.

82   "lurking devil in his sneer": From Byron's *Corsair* (1814). See also page 137.

82   "terror in his looks": *Romeo and Juliet,* act 3, scene 3.

82   "a tale unfold": *Hamlet,* act 1, scene 5.

83   "with what appetite": *Henry VIII,* act 3, scene 2.

83   "falsely so called": 1 Timothy 6:20–21: "O Timothy, keep that which is committed to thy trust, avoiding profane *and* vain babblings, and oppositions of science falsely so called: Which some professing have erred concerning the faith. Grace *be* with thee. Amen."

83   "grape and cannister": Anti-personnel artillery ammunition similar in design (though not in scale) to a shotgun shell.

83   *New Orleans, June 27:* This is the only entry in the series that asserts it was written in New Orleans at the time of its publication. Whitman or his editor is overcompensating; this piece is the first to appear after Whitman had returned to New York. It was either written in town and left with the *Crescent* or sent via mail.

Sketches of the Sidewalks and Levee: Old Benjamin Broekindown

83   "There is hardly any thing": The correct quote reads "There is *scarcely* anything that is really what it appears to be" and appears in Elbridge Gerry Paige's "On Delusion," one of his widely popular, humorous *Short Patent Sermons* (1845). Writing under the pseudonym "Dow Jr.," Paige (1818–1859) was primarily associated with New York papers like the *Sunday Mercury,*

which he owned and edited, before moving to the West Coast in the early 1850s. He died in San Francisco by suicide after a long struggle with alcohol addiction.

83   "dull, inferior clod": Exact source is unclear. "Inferior clod" could have been lifted from the hymn "My God, My Portion, and My Love" by Isaac Watts (1674–1749), where it refers to the earth. Whitman knew about Watts and noted the dates of his birth and death (alongside those of luminaries like Shakespeare, Pope, and Locke) in a notebook composed sometime between 1848 and 1856. Therein, Whitman praised Watts as "a dissenter" ("Autobiographical Data" notebook, Whitman Archive).

83   "Vanity of vanities": Ecclesiastes 1:2–11.

83   "lends the word of promise": *Macbeth:* act 5, scene 8: "That palter with us in a double sense; / That keep the word of promise to our ear, / And break it to our hope."

84   "La Guapa": "The Pretty (One)."

84   "monied aristocracy": A Jeffersonian term for bankers and speculators.

84   *agrarianism:* Another reference to Jeffersonianism. Jefferson opposed industrialization and envisioned a landed democracy of "yeoman farmers." The Whitmans—as the name of Walter's younger brother attests—were fervent Jeffersonians.

85   "keep soul and body together": Eighteenth-century expression, likely going back to John Adams.

85   "when pain and anguish": From Walter Scott's "Marmion" (1808).

86   "repair his fortune": *Othello,* act 2, scene 3.

86   "know by hear": Old saying, likely introduced into English by Chaucer.

86   "Man wants but little": One of the most famous quotes from the Romantic ballad *The Hermit* by Oliver Goldsmith (1728/1730–1774). Whitman had a keen interest in Goldsmith and would later take notes about the Irish writer's biography.

86   "Let him that thinketh": 1 Corinthians 10:12.

87   "Perhaps it may turn out": From Robert Burns's 1786 "Epistle to a Young Friend." See also page 143.

Sketches of the Sidewalks and Levee: Samuel Sensitive, Part I

88   "begotten him": Famous quote by one of the main characters in Sheridan's *The Rivals.* See also page 139.

88   "cut stick": To leave promptly; to go with all speed.

88   far-famed Dolbear: Thomas P. Dolbear, author of *The Science of Practical Penmanship* (New York: Collins, Keese, and Co., 1836), which proposed a system of "greatest rapidity" of handwriting, inspired by nervous science. Whitman was known for his beautiful and clear handwriting, which later helped him gain secretarial work. Even in old age he retained an interest in handwriting, guiding one of his young lovers, Harry Stafford, through exercises in penmanship.

88   "How happy's the soldier": From "How Happy the Soldier," a song popular with British soldiers during the Revolutionary War but adopted by the Americans and sung on both sides when they faced each other again during the War of 1812.

89   "Bliss beyond all": From the poem "The Light of the Haram" (1817) by Thomas Moore, often
      reprinted in wedding announcements or used to illustrate the bliss of marriage in sentimen-
      tal fiction.

89   "man proud man": *Measure for Measure,* act 2 scene 2.

89   "they took mighty good care": Exact source unknown, "crib" here means manger or fodder
      bin.

90   "And if our lot": "For if our stock be very small / 'Tis prudence to enjoy it all" from the poem
      "The Fireside" by Nathaniel Cotton (1702–1788).

90   Katydid: Katydids were often associated with women because of their song. That association
      was not always positive, as Oliver Wendell Holmes reminds us later in the century: "Thou
      art a female, Katydid! / I know it by the thrill / That quivers through thy piercing notes, / So
      petulant and shrill."

Sketches of the Sidewalks and Levee: Samuel Sensitive, Part II

90   Samuel Sensitive: This installment was the series' most popular entry, being quickly re-
      printed in a number of papers from New York to Georgia to Illinois.

91   morceau: A short composition, a song.

91   *bijouterie:* Pretty trinkets.

91   "made and provided": Alludes to statute law, suggesting everything is proceeding in an ap-
      propriate manner.

91   "'Twere long to tell": From William Wordsworth's posthumously published *The Prelude or,
      Growth of a Poet's Mind; An Autobiographical Poem* (1850). See also page 134.

91   mesmerism: Pseudoscientific electrophysiology. See also page 135.

91   gone hoss: A gone horse; that is, it was too late for him.

91   "imbrute": The term exists throughout Milton's work and describes a denigration towards
      brutishness. Here it is likely a reference to Milton's celebration of chastity, *Comus* (1634): "By
      unchaste looks, loose gestures, and foul talk, / But most by lewd and lavish act of sin, / Lets
      in defilement to the inward parts, / The soul grows clotted by contagion, / Imbodies, and
      imbrutes, till she quite loose / The divine property of her first being."

91   "twice blessed": *The Merchant of Venice,* act 4, scene 1.

91   "love darting eyes": The line, from Milton's *Comus,* reads: "Love-darting eyes, or tresses like
      the morn?"

92   "O meet me by the moonlight": Likely a reference to the popular song "Meet Me by Moon-
      light" (1830) by Irish composer Joseph Augustine Wade (1796–1845).

92   "Had we never loved": From "Ae Fond Kiss" (1791) by Robert Burns. See also page 143.

92   "stoned urn and monumental bust": "*Storied* urn and monumental bust" was a somewhat
      common literary expression at the time, and the line "storied urn or animated bust" is from
      the poem "Elegy Written in a Country Churchyard" by Thomas Grey (1751). It appears Whit-
      man is attempting to quote the poem from memory but committing a common mistake in
      doing so.

93   "His dream of life": From Thomas Moore's poem "Love's Young Dream."

93   Why lengthen the recital: Whitman tends to hasten through depictions of heterosexual

courtship and prefers to skip toward married bliss in a number of his major prose works, including *Jack Engle*.

Sketches of the Sidewalks and Levee: Miss Virginity Roseblossom

93 **solitary specimen of old maidism**: Whitman's vitriol in this sketch might come as a surprise, especially considering his generally positive depiction of women, including his veneration of mothers. Still, in his prose of the 1840s readers can discern a disgust with women who either refuse to be mothers or act unbecoming to their position as mother, be it the "solemn and sour" spinster of *Franklin Evans* (1842) or the "yellow-faced" spinster in "Shadow and the Light of a Young Man's Soul" (1848), written around the same time as this sketch, whose heartless ambition "spreads its bitterness over . . . families, and carries them through the spring and early summer of life with no inhalement of sweets, and no plucking of flowers!" (both texts at Whitman Archive).

94 **"summon spirits"**: *Henry IV,* Part 1, act 3, scene 1.

94 **"double, double, toil and trouble"**: *Macbeth,* act 4, scene 1.

94 **battle of Bladensburg**: One of the worst defeats of American troops by the British in the War of 1812.

95 **"pine in want"**: Common poetic phrase, for instance in James Thomson's (1700–1748) "A Man Perishing in the Snow: From Whence Reflections Are Raised on the Miseries of Life" (1726).

95 **"neither variableness, nor shadow"**: James 1:17.

95 **"the voice of the charmer"**: Psalm 58:5. Referring to a snake charmer.

95 **"sound of brass and tinkling jingle"**: 1 Corinthians 13:1–2.

96 **mesmerism**: Pseudoscientific electrophysiology. See also page 135.

96 **"flying artillery"**: Horse-drawn canons.

96 **dégoûtant**: French for "disgusting."

96 **lion and the lamb lying down**: A common, though incorrect, allusion to Isaiah 11:6. In the famous passage, the wolf lies down with the lamb and the lion with the calf.

97 **Mrs. Caudle spirit**: Mrs. Caudle was the fictional embodiment of the nagging wife, first appearing in the pages of *Punch* in 1845.

97 *love of sway:* Perhaps Whitman is referring to Dryden's (1631–1700) rendition of Chaucer's "Wife of Bath," in which the eponymous character exclaims: "This, at the peril of my head, I say, / A blunt plain truth, the sex aspires to sway." The phrase "love of sway" does not exist in Dryden's oeuvre. In Pope's *Epistles to Several Persons,* invoked elsewhere in Sidewalk Sketches, however, it does: "In women, two almost divide the kind; / Those, only fix'd, they first or last obey, / The love of pleasure, and the love of sway."

97 **"quality of mercy"**: *The Merchant of Venice,* act IV, scene 1.

97 **"It is vain"**: From Lord Byron's *Childe Harold's Pilgrimage* (1812–18). See also page 137.

97 **"envy, hatred, malice"**: From the *Book of Common Prayer.*

98 **"A lizard's body"**: From English poet James Merrick's (1720–1769) "The Chameleon." Whitman may have encountered it as an epigraph in James Fenimore Cooper's (1789–1851) *The Deerslayer* (1841). Whitman loved Cooper's early work and referenced characters from the

Leatherstocking series (among them *Deerslayer*) in his later *Brooklyniana* journalism. Whitman (re)read *Deerslayer* in the final years of his life and found it wanting: "It is inexpressibly dry to me; full of dialogue, full of long impossible speeches—at the end leaving you nowhere" (in Horace Traubel, *With Walt Whitman in Camden*, vol. 7, ed. Jeanne Chapman and Robert MacIsaac [Carbondale: Southern Illinois University Press, 1992], 4–5).

Sketches of the Sidewalks and Levee: Ephraim Broadhorn. A Flatboatman from Kentucky

98   **Flatboatman:** Flatboats were broad, low trading vessels. The whole scene that follows seems to echo Whitman's own impressions as much as "The Jolly Flatboatmen" by George Caleb Bingham, a painting Whitman had very likely seen, by a painter he admired. It even features the exact clothing items described here. See illustration on page 99. One can note a certain similarity between these figures and Whitman's portrait in the 1855 edition of *Leaves of Grass*.

99   **"Love their land":** From Fitz-Greene Halleck's (1790–1867) "Connecticut" (ca. 1820). It appears Whitman only created the narratively unnecessary youth of Broadhorn in Connecticut to be able to include these lines by the "American Byron" (as one biographer terms Halleck). The homosocial working-man's Republic depicted in the poem—"a pure republic, wild, yet strong, / A 'fierce democracie,' where all are true"—appealed to Whitman and is echoed in the Broadhorn sketch. Whitman would later socialize with Halleck at one of the main hangouts of the New York Bohême, Pfaff's Beer Cellar, and Halleck's sexual queerness likely had a major impact on his poetic and personal development. See also John W. M. Hallock's *The American Byron: Homosexuality and the Fall of Fitz-Greene Halleck* (Madison: University of Wisconsin Press, 2009).

100   **"more holy than righteous":** Popular saying of the mid-1800s and here a pun on holes in clothes.

100   **bran new:** Common, dialectic spelling of "brand new" that is also frequently seen in Dickens and Twain.

100   *omnium gatherum:* A miscellany of people or things.

101   **"This life is all":** An often-misquoted passage from the poem "Consolation" (1816) by Thomas Moore. It should read: "This world is all a fleeting show, / For man's illusion given."

101   **"feast of reason":** An intellectual debate. A common saying, originating in Pope's *Imitations of Horace* (1733–38).

101   **"home consumption":** Probably a reference to home-brewed, unregulated alcohol.

101   **"wet damnation":** While it is quoted by the famous essayist Lamb (1775–1834) in his "Confessions of a Drunkard," this phrase originates in act 3, part 1, of the Jacobean revenge drama *The Revenger's Tragedy* (ca. 1606) then falsely attributed to Cyril Tourneur.

101   **"to see the elephant":** A popular expression at the time that likely originated as a reference to England's first zoo (and the phrase "to see the lion") and was adapted in the United States in reference to its first elephant exhibit. It means: to gain worldliness by great expense.

102   "C' est la même chose": "It's the same thing." Whitman did not speak French. Undeterred by that fact, he frequently used French words and phrases, often misspelled, in his journalistic and poetic work. Whitman had, as Roger Asselineau puts it, a life-long fascination with French as the "language of popular, dynamism" and democratic revolutions ("Foreign Language Borrowings," *Walt Whitman: An Encyclopedia* ed. J. R. LeMaster and Donald D. Kummings [New York: Garland Publishing, 1998], 228, in Whitman Archive).

102   "Qu'est—ce que c'est?": "What—What is that?"

102   "vous etes mystère": "You're a mystery."

102   *la Rue Royale:* Royal Street in the French Quarter.

102   "A stubborn race": From Halleck's "Connecticut." See also page 152.

103   "View them near": Halleck's "Connecticut" again. See also page 152.

103   "the unsophisticated good sense": Whitman ends his series on an expressly political note. This quote is by William Pinkney (1764–1822), an influential Democratic-Republican politician from Maryland. It is taken from his defense of the 1820 "Missouri Compromise," a piece of legislation he helped draft, which admitted Missouri as a slave state and Maine as a free state. Pinkney's plea to respect the "the unsophisticated good sense and noble spirit of the American people" makes a state-based "popular sovereignty" argument (claiming that the people of each new state should be allowed the same right to decide whether to be a slave state or not).

EPILOGUE: MEMORIES OF NEW ORLEANS

Manuscript Fragment about New Orleans

104   H. and M'C: The editors, Alexander Hamilton Hayes (1806–1866) and John Eliot McClure (ca. 1819–1869).

104   Jef.: Whitman's brother, Thomas Jefferson Whitman (1833–1890), who was named, like his brothers Andrew Jackson (1827–1863) and George Washington (1829–1901), after what Whitman's father considered to be republican heroes.

105   Mr. Larue: John C. Larue (ca. 1810–1856), who later became a judge. Contrary to Whitman's assessment, Larue and his writings appear to have been rather unpopular. Even one of his obituaries felt the need to criticize his demeanor, noting that "[t]here was in his writings, as in his manners, a repulsive cynicism" (*Feliciana Democrat*, November 22, 1856).

105   Mr. Reeder: George W. Reeder (ca. 1822–1848), an actor and prose writer. He died of cholera only days after his brother had succumbed to the same disease ("George W. Reeder," *Daily Crescent*, December 27, 1848).

105   DaPonte: Durant DaPonte (1830–1894), descended from a family of opera singers, who contributed poems and translations to the *Crescent* and would quickly rise the ranks after Whitman's departure.

105   I packed up my traps: The rest of the note is not extant.

New Orleans in 1848

106   not the *Picayune:* Alexander Hayes, coeditor of the *Crescent,* had been foreman at the *Picayune* in his youth. There, he met the young counting-room clerk John E. McClure. The two would go on to found first the *Delta* and then the *Crescent* ("John E. McClure," *Times-Picayune,* May 16, 1869).

106   "Chapparal": A Mexican correspondent (correctly spelled "Chaparral"), known for his war coverage. "Chaparral" was John H. Peoples of the *Corpus Christi Star;* see "The Corpus Christi Expedition," *New Orleans Weekly Delta,* September 25, 1848.

106   Gen. Taylor with his staff: See Whitman's "General Taylor at the Theatre" in appendix B.

106   "Model Artists": See page 135 and Whitman's editorial on the "Model Artists" in appendix B.

106   Gen. Pillow: Gideon Johnson Pillow (1806–1878), a major general during the Mexican American War, who was in the news during Whitman's time in New Orleans for the charge of claiming undue credit for the American victory. He beat the accusation, which almost resulted in a court-martial, with the assistance of President Polk.

107   coffee: After some initial health concerns about "hot drinks" (expressed in his "Sun-Down Papers" of 1840), Whitman came to love coffee in all its forms, including in cakes. "[C]offee carries with it decided esthetic satisfactions," he told a close associate later in life (quote from Horace Traubel, *With Walt Whitman in Camden,* vol. 4, ed. Sculley Bradley [Philadelphia: University of Pennsylvania Press, 1953, 16]). Newspaper clippings of coffee cakes have survived in Whitman's notebooks; the recipe can be found in Gary Scharnhorst's *Literary Eats* (Jefferson, LA: McFarland & Co, 2014), 192.

107   old Catholic Cathedral: Today's St. Louis Cathedral.

109   Montauk voyage, East Long Island: Whitman visited Montauk Point in mid-September of 1847, which causes him to reflect on the aboriginal nature of the place in a letter to the *Brooklyn Daily Eagle* ("East Long Island Correspondence," September 20, 1847). See also Whitman's poem "From Montauk Point" in the final edition of *Leaves of Grass.*

110   Hunker: Term for the conservative forces of the Democratic party, so named for the "hankering" for federal office at the cost of Democratic principles.

APPENDIX A: LETTERS FROM THOMAS JEFFERSON ("JEFF") WHITMAN TO HIS FAMILY

Mid-February: Trip to New Orleans and First Impressions

117   Father: Walter Whitman Sr. (1789–1855), an alcoholic carpenter and failed real-estate speculator. The relationship between Whitman senior and junior was strained, but Walt certainly inherited his father's love for working-class Democratic ideology.

118   Mother: Louisa Van Velsor Whitman (1795–1873), adored by Walt and a template for his view of women.

118   Astor house: The Astor House, which had opened in 1838, was a major hotel on the corner of Broadway and Vesey. Whitman considered the "simple, square, unornamented architecture

of the Astor House . . . the best appearance of any building in New York" ("Letters from New York," *National Era*, November 14, 1850).

March 14: Employment at the Crescent *and City Perambulations*

119 **eighth or ninth letter:** Those letters excerpted here are the only extant letters.

119 **Mr. Wilson in the *Eagle* office:** The paper Whitman left to work at the *Crescent*. Whitman likely retained a working relationship with the paper's owners. The *Eagle* praised the first edition of the *Crescent* and reprinted some of Whitman's work from it. Dennis Berthold and Kenneth M. Price (for the Whitman Archive) suggest that Mr. Wilson was "Peter W. Wilson, a printer." Wilson also contributed correspondence to the *Crescent* during Whitman's tenure, signing it "P.W.W."

119 ***five* dollars per week:** In terms of buying power, roughly equivalent to $165 today.

119 **sister Mary's visit:** Mary Elizabeth Van Nostrand (1821–1899), Walt Whitman's younger sister, who had moved to Greenport, Long Island, in 1840 with her shipbuilder husband.

120 **next door to the Theatre:** "Next door" in the mid-1800s meant "close and on the same side of the road." Tremont House was indeed two blocks to the west of the St. Charles Theater.

120 **old Catholic cemetery:** Likely Saint Louis Cemetery, which opened in 1789, roughly twenty minutes by foot to the north of Whitman's lodgings.

120 **old French church:** St. Louis Cathedral, which the elder Whitman also mentions in his writings.

120 **George and Andrew:** His brothers Andrew Jackson Whitman (1827–1863), nicknamed "Bunkum" for his chronic health issues, and George Washington Whitman (1829–1901), who would be wounded during the Civil War, causing Walt to move to Washington, DC, to find him—which marked the beginning of the poet's interest in caring for the war wounded and led to the creation of his "Good Gray Poet" persona.

120 **Mr. Collins:** John Collins, "the celebrated Irish Comedian," performed on St. Patrick's Day at Armory Hall, performing some of his hits like "Birth of St. Patrick" and "Widow Machree" ("St. Patrick's Day," *Daily Crescent*, March 17, 1848).

120 **Sister Hannah:** Hannah Louisa Whitman (1823–1908), Walt's younger sister and one of his favorite correspondents in later life. She attended seminary and taught school during the time of Jefferson's letters. Hannah slipped into poverty when she married the abusive landscape artist Charles Heyde, who ultimately died in an insane asylum. Hannah would be buried next to Walt.

121 **Eddy:** Edward Whitman (1835–1892), the youngest son of the Whitman family, received special care throughout his life for various mental and physical disabilities, including epilepsy. During his final period of declining health, "Eddy" was institutionalized. In the last meeting of the two Whitman brothers, they held hands in silence. Walt, who had supported Edward financially throughout his life, made him the primary beneficiary of his will.

March 27: Daily Life

121   a very fine public park: Lafayette Square.

122   "flounces": An exaggerated, overly expressive way of moving.

APPENDIX B: ADDITIONAL EDITORIALS

General Taylor at the Theatre

125   Maj. Gens. Taylor and Pillow: Future president Zachary Taylor (1784–1850), admired by Whitman for his heroism in the war. Still, Whitman remained skeptical of Taylor's qualifications for the presidency. Pillow: See page 154.

126   "Circassian Slaves": Circassian women (from the northwestern Caucasus) were believed to be the embodiment of beauty in the long nineteenth century as well as the focus of many orientalist paintings and sculptures.

126   hero of Buena Vista: During the battle of Buena Vista (in February 1847), Taylor's troops held back, and ultimately forced the retreat of, a significantly more numerous Mexican attack due largely to superior US artillery.

A Question of Propriety

126   John Bull: The rotund personification of Great Britain, its equivalent to Uncle Sam.

University Studies

128   University of the State: The University of Louisiana, chartered in 1847, was located between Common Street and Canal Street on today's Roosevelt Way. It was privatized later in the century and became Tulane University.

128   Common School: Whitman was a former educator himself and vocally defended the Common School idea (as opposed to private or religious schools) in his journalistic work.

129   "If God held in his right hand": From Gotthold Ephraim Lessing's (1729–1761) enlightenment work *Anti-Goeze* (1778). Among Whitman's notebooks are annotations of texts on Lessing, and he would frequently evoke the poet-philosopher in discussions with his disciples.

130   Story and Kent: Likely US Supreme Court Justice Joseph Story (1779–1845) and legal scholar James Kent (1763–1847).

130   Mr. Peters' Essays: A book by this title does not appear to exist. Perhaps, "Mr. Peters" is businessman Samuel Jarvis Peters (1801–1855), the founder of the public-school system of New Orleans and the president of its chamber of commerce. Peters was an outspoken Whig and was rumored, in 1848, to be in play for the position of secretary of the treasury in President Taylor's (Whig) cabinet. Instead he became the collector of customs at the port of New Orleans in the following year. The Whigs strongly supported tariffs—which Barnburner

Whitman opposed. To Whitman, implementing "the favorite Whig measures [of] a national bank, high tariff, funding of the state debts, and such like" meant "throwing . . . monstrously unequal amounts of wealth into the possession of a select few" ("A Word to Our 'Native' Friends," *Brooklyn Daily Eagle,* August 4, 1846).

WHITMAN'S BIBLIOGRAPHY UNTIL 1848

Contributions to papers include reviews, editorials, poems, peeps, and news items. Short stories and novellas, as well as named journalistic series, are listed separately. Whitman's early fiction was frequently reprinted, which may be traced in the fiction bibliography maintained by Stephanie M. Blalock for the Whitman Archive.

1834–39 Contributes to *New York Mirror, Long Islander, Universalist Union*

1840   Contributes to *Hempstead Inquirer, Long Island Democrat*
        "Sun-Down Papers" series (*Hempstead Inquirer, Long-Island Democrat*, and *Long-Island Farmer*)

1841   Contributes to *Long Island Famer*
        "Death in the School-Room. A Fact" (*United States Magazine and Democratic Review*)
        "Wild Frank's Return" (*United States Magazine and Democratic Review*)
        "The Child's Champion" (*New World* and *Columbian Lady's and Gentleman's Magazine*)
        "Bervance: or, Father and Son" (*United States Magazine and Democratic Review*)

1842   Contributes to *Brother Jonathan, New York Aurora, Sunday Times, Evening Tattler, New World, Sun, Daily Plebeian, New Era*
        "The Tomb-Blossoms" (*United States Magazine and Democratic Review*)
        "The Last of the Sacred Army" (*United States Magazine and Democratic Review*)
        "The Child-Ghost" (*United States Magazine and Democratic Review*)
        "Reuben's Last Wish" (*Washingtonian*)
        "A Legend of Life and Love" (*United States Magazine and Democratic Review*)
        "The Angel of Tears" (*United States Magazine and Democratic Review*)

Franklin Evans; or, the Inebriate (*New World* and *Brooklyn Daily Eagle*)
"The Reformed" (*New York Sun* and *Brooklyn Daily Eagle*)
"Lingave's Temptation" (*New-York Observer*)

1843   Contributes to *Sun, Daily Plebeian, Subterranean, Brother Jonathan*
        "The Madman" (*New York Washingtonian and Organ*)
        "The Love of the Four Students" (*New Mirror*)

1844   Contributes to *Sunday Times, New York Democrat, New York Sunday Times and*
            Noah's Weekly
        "Eris; A Spirit Record" (*Columbian Lady's and Gentleman's Magazine*)
        "The Little Sleighers" (*Columbian Lady's and Gentleman's Magazine*)
        "My Boys and Girls" (*Rover*)
        "The Fireman's Dream" (*New York Sunday Times and Noah's Weekly Messenger*)
        "Dumb Kate.—An Early Death" (*Columbian Lady's and Gentleman's Magazine*)

1845   Contributes to *Broadway Journal, United States Magazine, American Review,*
            Brooklyn Evening Star
        "Arrow-Tip" / "The Half-Breed" (*Aristidean* and *United States Magazine and*
            Democratic Review)
        "Shirval: A Tale of Jerusalem" (*Aristidean*)
        "Richard Parker's Widow" (*Aristidean*)
        "Revenge and Requital; A Tale of a Murderer Escaped" (*United States Magazine*
            and Democratic Review and *Brooklyn Daily Eagle*)
        "Some Fact-Romances" (*Aristidean*)

1846   Contributes to *Brooklyn Evening Star, Brooklyn Daily Eagle*

1847   Contributes to *Brooklyn Daily Eagle*

1848   Contributes to *Brooklyn Daily Eagle, Daily Crescent, Brooklyn Weekly Freeman*
        "Sketches from the Sidewalks and the Levee" series (*Daily Crescent*)
        "The Shadow and the Light of a Young Man's Soul" (*Union Magazine of Liter-*
            ature and Art)

RECOMMENDED
FURTHER READING

Bethel, Denise. "Notes on an Early Daguerreotype of Walt Whitman." *Walt Whitman Quarterly Review* 9 (Winter 1992): 148–53. https://doi.org/10.13008/2153-3695.1327.

Blalock, Stephanie M. "Periodical Fiction." In *Walt Whitman in Context,* ed. Levin and Whitley.

Cohen, Matt. "The American South." In *Walt Whitman in Context,* ed. Levin and Whitley.

Erkkila, Betsy. *Walt Whitman's Songs of Male Intimacy and Love: "Live Oak, with Moss" and "Calamus."* Iowa City: University of Iowa Press, 2011. Walt Whitman Archive.

Folsom, Ed. "What New Orleans Meant to Walt Whitman." *New Orleans: A Literary History,* ed. T. R. Johnson. Cambridge, UK: Cambridge University Press, 2019.

Harris, Maverick Marvin. "Democratic Party," "New Orleans Crescent," "New Orleans, Louisiana," "New Orleans Picayune." In *Walt Whitman: An Encyclopedia,* ed. J. R. LeMaster and Donald D. Kummings. New York: Garland, 1998. Walt Whitman Archive.

Levin, Joanna, and Edward Whitley, eds. *Walt Whitman in Context.* Cambridge, UK: Cambridge University Press, 2018.

McMullen, Kevin, Jason Stacy, and Stefan Schöberlein. "Walt Whitman at the *Aurora:* A Model for Journalistic Attribution." *Walt Whitman Quarterly Review* 37 (Summer–Fall 2019): 107–15. https://doi.org/10.13008/0737-0679.2362.

Noverr, Douglas A., and Jason Stacy, eds. *Walt Whitman's Selected Journalism.* Iowa City: University of Iowa Press, 2015.

Schöberlein, Stefan, and Zachary Turpin. "'Glorious Times for Newspaper Editors and Correspondents': Whitman at the New Orleans *Daily Crescent,* 1848–1849." *Walt Whitman Quarterly* 39 (Summer 2021): 1–39. https://doi.org/10.13008/0737-0679.2414.

Stacy, Jason. "Journalism." In *Walt Whitman in Context,* ed. Levin and Whitley.

———. *Walt Whitman's Multitudes: Labor Reform and Persona in Whitman's Journalism and the First Leaves of Grass, 1840–1855.* New York: Peter Lang, 2008.

The Uncollected Poetry and Prose of Walt Whitman, Much of Which Has Been but Recently Discovered. 2 vols. Ed. Emory Holloway. New York: P. Smith, 1932.

Walt Whitman Archive. Ed. Matt Cohen, Ed Folsom, and Kenneth M. Price. www.whitman archive.org.

Wilson, Ivy G., ed. *Whitman Noir: Black America and the Good Gray Poet.* Iowa City: University of Iowa Press, 2014. Walt Whitman Archive.

INDEX